The Crisis of the In

The Crisis of the Inner City

Edited by

Martin Loney

and

Mark Allen

© Mark Allen, Ron Bailey, Bob Davis, Judith
Green, Bill Jordan, Martin Loney, Alex Lyon,
Marjorie Mayo, Jef Smith, Robin Thompson,
Andrew Thornley, John Tilley, Peter Walker,
Jean Whitfield 1979

First published 1979 by
THE MACMILLAN PRESS LTD
London and Basingstoke
Associated companies in Delhi Dublin
Hong Kong Johannesburg Lagos Melbourne
New York Singapore and Tokyo

Printed and bound in Great Britain by
REDWOOD BURN LIMITED
Trowbridge & Esher.

British Library Cataloguing in Publication Data

The crisis of the inner city.
   1. Cities and towns—Great Britain
   2. Great Britain—Social conditions—1945-
  I. Loney, Martin   II. Allen, Mark
  309. 1'41   HT133

  ISBN 0-333-25690-5
  ISBN 0-333-25691-3 Pbk

Contents

Preface

In inviting contributions to this volume the editors have been concerned to provide a variety of perspectives on what is popularly termed the inner city crisis. In particular the volume is addressed not simply to students and academics but also, and primarily, to practitioners. It is directed at those who as politicians, administrators, professionals or activists make, implement or oppose policies which affect the inner city.

Our concern is to clarify both the nature of the inner city crisis and the kinds of responses which are open. The solutions must be found by those who live and work in the inner city, and it is ultimately their strength and their ability to fight for decent conditions which will determine the outcome. We hope this volume will, in some small measure, be of assistance.

We would like to thank Carol Johns for her help in preparing the manuscripts for the publishers.

December 1978   M. L.
                                                                     M. A.

Notes on Contributors

MARK ALLEN is Editor in Chief of *Community Care* and Editor of *Nursing Mirror*.

RON BAILEY has worked in the housing field since 1965. He is currently working for the Housing Emergency Office. His publications include *The Squatters* (Penguin, 1973) and *The Homeless and the Empty Houses* (Penguin, 1977). He wrote *The Grief Report* for Shelter in 1972.

BOB DAVIS worked as a Research Fellow at Newcastle-upon-Tyne Polytechnic and the North Tyneside Community Development Project from 1973-8. He is currently employed as a community worker at the Walker Resource Centre, Newcastle-upon-Tyne.

JUDITH GREEN was a Research Fellow with the University of Durham and the Benwell (Newcastle) Community Development Project from 1974-8. She is currently employed as a local government research officer.

BILL JORDAN is a Lecturer in Social Work at Exeter University and a part-time social worker at Exe Vale Hospital, Exeter. His publications include *Paupers* (Routledge and Kegan Paul, 1973) and *Poor Parents* (Routledge and Kegan Paul, 1974).

MARTIN LONEY lectures in Social Policy at the Open University. He has served as Director of Research for World University Service in Geneva and as General Secretary of the National Council for Civil Liberties. His previous publications include *Rhodesia: White Racism and Imperial Response* (Penguin, 1975).

ALEX LYON, MP, has represented York since 1966. He was Minister of State at the Home Office, 1974-6.

MARJORIE MAYO works with the Joint Docklands Action Group. She previously worked with the Community Development Project central research team and lectured at the University of Surrey. She has published extensively on community work and edited *Women in the Community* (Routledge and Kegan Paul, 1977).

JEF SMITH is Director of Social Services for Kingston-upon-Thames. His articles have appeared in *New Society*, *Community Care* and *Social Work Today*.

ROBIN THOMPSON is Deputy Borough Planning Officer for the London Borough of Greenwich. He has worked at the Centre for Environmental Studies and the Architectural Association and is a council member of the Royal Town Planning Institute.

ANDREW THORNLEY lectures in Planning at the Polytechnic of Central London. His publications include *Theoretical Perspectives on Planning Participation* (Pergamon, 1977).

JOHN TILLEY, MP, represents Lambeth Central. He was formerly council leader in the London Borough of Wandsworth.

PETER WALKER, MBE, MP, has represented Worcester since 1961. He became the first Secretary of State for the Environment in 1971, and subsequently served as Secretary of State for Trade and Industry. His recent publications include *The Ascent of Britain* (Sidgwick and Jackson, 1977).

JEAN WHITFIELD grew up in South-east London and is now an unemployed married woman. She is a member of the Plymouth Claimants Union.

Introduction

Martin Loney

> If, in this country, democracy falls, it will fall, not through
> any fortuitous combination of unfriendly circumstances,
> but from the insincerity of some of its professed defenders,
> and the timidity of the remainder. It will fall because,
> when there was still time to make it unassailable, public
> spirit was too weak, and class egotism too strong, for the
> opportunity to be seized. If it stands, it will stand, not
> because it has hitherto stood, but because ordinary men
> and women were determined that it should, and threw
> themselves with energy into broadening its foundations.
> To broaden its foundations means, in the conditions of
> today, to destroy plutocracy and to set in its place an
> equalitarian society.[1]
>
> R. H. Tawney

It is over a decade since Harold Wilson announced his urban
programme from the steps of Birmingham Town Hall. In that
time government expenditure on special programmes directed
to the inner city has increased more than twentyfold. Yet in
spite of this increase there are few who would argue that
inner city residents are better off today than they were
before the programme was launched.

Some commentators have argued that inner city decline is
inevitable, reflecting both the changing economy and a
growing preference for suburban life. For this school government action should be limited to easing the transition and

cushioning the inner cities' more vulnerable residents against the worst effects of decay. Others have argued that vigorous government policies or alternatively, in the free market model, a reduction in government regulation could turn the inner city areas into centres of vigorous enterprise either through such expedients as trade marts or through a revival of small business activity and the continued growth of the service sector.

Government thinking has evolved from the narrow focus on the assumed negative characteristics of inner city residents—the social pathology approach which underlay the Community Development Projects—to an awareness of the centrality of employment prospects for inner city recovery. The Department of the Environment through the Inner Urban Areas Act, which provides among other things for subsidies for industrial building, has demonstrated a commitment to reversing previous government policy by encouraging industry to return to the city rather than supporting further decentralisation. The Department of the Environment's strategy relies on a substantial shift of manufacturing industry into the inner city but there is no evidence that either the Department of Industry or the National Exterprise Board is backing such a policy.

The partnership authorities have committed little of their funds to employment projects. This may well be justified since the relatively small sums at their disposal can be better spent in improving the social provisions for local residents rather that engaging in an unequal, and probably unsuccessful, struggle to attract large firms back to the inner city. In a context of rising national unemployment, which may be rapidly accelerated by the use of microprocessors, the prospects for increasing inner city employment look bleak. In the next decade the automation of routine office work may well diminish inner city clerical jobs as rapidly, as, in the past, blue-collar jobs disappeared.

In the face of the enormous problems of the inner cities the amounts of money spent under various aspects of the urban programme remain trifling even though their apparent magnitude has risen dramatically. In early 1979 a small further increase in expenditure on inner city programmes was announced by the Department of the Environment but in reality should have been offset against a staggering under-spending of more than £400 million on housing, by the same department. In many areas adequate housing is desperately needed but the number of new council houses begun has fallen from 170,800 in 1976 to 107,600 in 1978. For all the special programmes it is arguable that the inner cities still remain disadvantaged in terms of central government spend-ing, which through the 'needs assessment' of the rates support grant has provided much higher subsidies to the wealthier suburbs than to inner city areas. Between 1974/5 and 1977/8 the grant to the inner London borough of Tower Hamlets rose by 33.9 per cent but the grant to Sutton, in the more affluent commuter belt, rose by 72.2 per cent.

Whatever the merits of particular aspects of the inner city programme it has been conducted against a backcloth of continual economic decline which has placed the greatest burden on the weakest sectors. Britain's *per capita* income is now below that of East Germany, while its distribution remains far more unequal. Manufacturing output hovers at the level achieved under Heath's three-day week. Government job-creation programmes proliferate but many inner city school-leavers, disadvantaged by virtue of home background, education or racialism, are unlikely to compete successfully for worthwhile jobs.

The position of the low paid has further declined. In April 1975 the lowest 10 per cent of male workers were earning 65.2 per cent of the average wage. In April 1978 they were earning 64.6 per cent. This small decline underestimates the real change in the position of the low paid since inflation struck basic commodities, notably foodstuffs, with particular severity, disproportionately reducing the real spending power of those on low incomes.

An inner city programme which is not part of a general strategy to combat social injustice can have little effect, a point made forcefully by many of the contributors to this volume. There is no evidence in the activities of any of the main political parties of any committment to such a strategy. Indeed, if anything, the trend in Britain is to greater inequality and the destruction of those fraternal and egalitarian impulses which used to provide some support for beleaguered working-class communities. Today the low paid are paraded as selfish vandals who are bringing the country to its knees. Racialism permeates every aspect of national life under the benign view of a Home Secretary whose immigration staff conduct regular indignities on black immigrants. Haphazard make-work programmes go hand in hand with government subsidies for the rapid, but unplanned, introduction of employment-reducing computer technology. With no realistic programme to tackle rising unemployment or social inequalities, government policies in the inner city are destined to have a marginal effect.

In the absence of any national strategy to combat social injustice, or indeed of any manifest concern with social injustice, it is difficult to see the inner city programme as anything more than a rather feeble response to growing concerns about social disorder. On the one hand the programme attracts a great deal of public attention, sustains the belief that government is tackling the problem and occupies us with the prospect of improvement, thus averting our eyes from the reality of decay. On the other hand faced by rising crime rates and increasing racial tension the inner city programme can provide a flexible means of injecting scarce resources into particularly sensitive areas. There is no doubt that the concern for social disorder is realistic, for, while British cities have not yet experienced the problems of American cities, in the words of W. H. Auden, 'those to whom evil is done, do evil in return'.[2]

There are nonetheless ways in which the inner city problem could be tackled; the resources are within our grasp. Between 1970 and 1976 the top 25 companies increased their profits by 70 per cent, though the rate of tax paid declined. In 1977 many of the top companies, including GKN, Ford, Courtaulds, Reed International, Esso and Rio Tinto Zinc, paid no profits tax. While increasing numbers of low-paid workers became liable to personal taxation, corporate profits provided a declining share of UK tax revenue. In 1976 they provided only 4.7 per cent of total tax revenue in contrast to most other western countries. In Japan, for example, taxes on corporate profits in the same year provided 39 per cent of total revenue.

The cutbacks in the social services which have undermined much of the impact of the inner city programmes have not been matched by cutbacks in the defence budget. Indeed, as the poor were being urged to make do with 5 per cent, the 1979 Defence White Paper envisaged an increase in military spending from £6919 million to £8500 million, an increase of nearly 24 per cent.

As I write this introduction the Socialist Minister of Transport, Williams Rogers, regrets that free public transport cannot be offered to the elderly and disabled since this would cost £200 million a year, and the Sixth Duke of Westminster a young ex-Etonian of 26, inherits his father's title to accompany the £500 million already passed to him. The money entrusted to this meritorious young man matches the total amount spent on Britain's inner city programmes in more than a decade.

Part 1
The Political Framework

1

A Conservative View

Peter Walker

The city is the most important of our products. It was
Winston Churchill who once said, 'We shape our cities and
then they shape our way of life'. Britain's urban problems are
aggravated because of the way the majority of our cities
developed in the early stages of the Industrial Revolution.
These cities contain old housing, old factories and old civic
buildings. Their rivers have been allowed to become polluted
and they suffer from a lack of any total concept or vision.
The western world faces problems that arise because a society
with a disorganised mixture of competing objectives is unable
to provide a high quality of life. The several self-interests do
not add up to common benefit. It is the way we tackle the
problem of improving the quality of city life that will determine whether our cities will prove to be the death or the
revival of our civilisation.

The despair of the deprived

The people who live in the most deprived areas of our major
cities have a bad record of voting, perhaps because over the
years they have felt that voting for one party or another did
not make very much difference. In these areas communica-
tions are bad: many of the people do not read widely, they
do not listen to the news programmes, and they concentrate
upon lighter entertainment if they have television. They do

not feel they have much power to influence authority, for what complaints they have made in past years have sometimes been listened to but seldom acted upon. The officers of local authorities and government departments appear to them rather remote, both physically and culturally. They have reached a stage of permanent despair in which there is little hope, and as hope disappears tacit acceptance takes its place.

Ignorance of the facts

I was not only the first Secretary of State for the Environment in Britain but the first person to hold such a position in any democracy, and I was excited by the possibility of using the resources of a large department to improve radically the condition of our inner city areas. I quickly discovered that the realities of inner city life in Britain were relatively unknown to both local and central government: it was known how many people were on social security in certain localities; there was an awareness of areas of high unemployment and areas where the crime rate was high; but there were no plans to transform these areas.

Primarily, there had been no assessment of what was necessary to improve housing conditions. Certain areas were scheduled demolition, a process that tended to add to a locality's misery for a considerable period of time. The bulldozer was used not just on houses that needed to be replaced but on countless thousands of houses that could well have been improved and would have provided far pleasanter houses than the multi-storey blocks to which their occupants were transferred. There was no accurate information about those people who needed social security and other benefits but were not obtaining them. There was no basic measure of the horrific conditions that currently existed or of the quality of life that it was so desperately important to obtain. I was determined to discover the scope of the problems and then to pursue policies that would transform the reality of today, ghastly and awful as it is for many communities, into a decent and tolerable life in the future.

The inner city studies

I decided to examine the underlying problems in six urban areas. Three of these areas were to be complete towns—Sunderland, Rotherham and Oldham—and three of them districts of major cities which were known to suffer from multiple deprivations—Liverpool 7 and 8, Birmingham Small Heath and the London borough of Lambeth. I decided that this was not an inquiry that should be in the hands of officials, because I felt that it was important that from the very beginning politicians, and politicians with power, should be immersed in the study. I asked that each of these inquiries should be under a steering committee of three people: a minister from my department, the leader of the local council (being the person with most political power in the locality concerned) and a senior partner of a major firm of consultants on urban problems. I took the chair at the inquiry looking into a district of Birmingham. Other of my ministers took the chair at each of the other inquiries. The six leaders of the councils agreed to take their place, and six different firms of consultants were chosen so that we would get a genuine diversity of ideas, observations and solutions from the reports. The store of knowledge thus obtained would enable us to tackle vigorously and competently the problems of our cities.

It is a matter of deep personal regret that within a few months of starting these studies I was moved to another department to become the Secretary of State for Trade and Industry. I regret even more that, thereafter, these studies took a lower priority in the work of the Department of the Environment. Ministerial interest gradually lessened and when the reports finally appeared, with little publicity or comment, they remained almost totally unknown, not only in the country as a whole but even in the towns and localities upon which the reports were based. Nevertheless, they have provided a fund of knowledge for future ministers to draw upon, for they do show the way to future progress, and even more devastatingly they point out the terrible mistakes of the past and the present, demonstrating clearly our continuing failure to provide the resources that are needed.

The greater the problem the less the help

The Liverpool study covers a district that has all the problems associated with the worst of our inner city areas—the district known as Liverpool 8. Liverpool 8 contains 9.6 per cent of the population of the city but it has a much higher incidence of the worst urban problems. At a time when the city was suffering from an unemployment rate of 8 per cent, Liverpool 8 had a rate of 11 per cent and the worst ward a rate of 18 per cent. Whereas 4 per cent of the population of Liverpool as a whole are immigrants, Liverpool 8 has 8 per cent and the worst ward 13 per cent. Liverpool has a far greater concentration of families with large numbers of children. In Liverpool as a whole 6 per cent of the families have more than four children. In Liverpool 8 the figure is 9 per cent. The number of educationally subnormal children in the worst district of Liverpool 8 is almost twice the figure for Liverpool as a whole. The proportion of adults who are mentally ill in the city as a whole is 0.5 per cent: in Liverpool 8 it is 2.8 per cent, in the worst ward 4.5 per cent.

The housing conditions in Liverpool 8 are very much worse than in the rest of the city. There are over 1.5 persons to a room in only 3 per cent of the households in Liverpool, but in the worst ward of Liverpool 8 the figure is 9 per cent. In the city as a whole 71 per cent of the population have a bath, an inside toilet and hot water, but only 43 per cent of the people in Liverpool 8 have such fundamental facilities. As to the housing stock in the area, 8 per cent is either due for clearance or has been scheduled as having a short life of only 15 years or less. Future plans for redevelopment will result in the closure of over 100 of the 180 businesses in the district.

With 9.6 per cent of the total population of Liverpool living in an area of such multi-deprivation, one would anticipate that much more than 9.6 per cent of Liverpool's expenditure would be put into the area. The inner city study discloses the horrifying fact that in this part of Liverpool they do not even obtain the 9.6 per cent of the expenditure which they would get if they were just getting the average allocation for the city as a whole, for they obtain only 6.1

per cent of the money available. The basic principle of the greater the problems the less the effort is, I am afraid, typical of many of Britain's cities.

The facts of Inner London

The first task in tackling our inner city problem is to ascertain the facts. Let us have a look at some of the basic facts concerning the Inner London area:

Number of households	1,120,000
Number of households occupied by council tenants	2 in 7
Number of households with someone on social security	1 in 6
Number of households with no bathroom	1 in 7
Number of households with no inside toilet	1 in 12
Number of households where there is a one-parent family	1 in 12
Number of households where there is someone suffering from a substantial permanent physical handicap	1 in 18

There are other terrifying facts. In the Inner London area there are some 12,000 children who have been taken from their parents into the care of the local authorities. The incidence of mental illness is very high. In the Inner London area in 1975 alone, 14,000 people were discharged from hospital after being treated for mental illness.

The crime figures for our cities are alarming, and accelerating. In the Inner London area in 1973 one in every 25 children between the ages of 10 and 16 was arrested. This proportion has grown worse since. In 1975 in the Metropolitan Police area young people between the ages of 10 and 16 accounted for half the arrests for burglary and a third of all the arrests.

The accelerating decline

What are the underlying problems that create these conditions? There is the growing problem of unemployment, a problem that increases as our public transport system breaks down. Many lower income families living in inner city areas are unable to provide their own transport, and as public transport ceases to function they become immobile. A second problem is the crime rate itself, for not only is it increasing and self-reinforcing but it creates further problems which encourage delinquency. It is very difficult to attract new businesses to areas of high crime rate. Businesses that are perpetually burgled and have to have windows barricaded find other locations. More people become unemployed and the crime rate rises. This particularly affects young people.

These districts contain a large proportion of elderly people who have nowhere else to move to and are trapped in the locality. They are the reception areas for those who move to our bigger cities, be it from Glasgow, Cork or Bombay. They are areas where there is very little proper professional advice available. The best solicitors do not site their offices in such localities, so the quality of legal advice is inferior. Doctors prefer to live and work in pleasant areas rather than where their professional skills are most needed.

Fundamental to the improvement of life in our inner cities is the task of creating better job opportunities. A combination of high unemployment and low earnings brings about a rapid deterioration in the quality of life in these areas. As jobs become scarce longer journeys are needed to obtain work, and as public transport breaks down job opportunities are reduced. As the price of public transport increases the expense of travelling considerable distances become a factor in still further reducing living standards. The necessity for mothers to work longer to supplement the family income means that the children receive less attention and the likelihood that children will play truant and commit petty crimes is correspondingly increased. The prospects of employment and good earnings are worse for the unskilled than the skilled, worse for black than white, worse for the school-leaver than those already established in their jobs. The inner city areas contain, predominantly, the unskilled and the blacks, and they also have a very substantial volume of school-leavers in proportion to their total populations. The difference between the aspirations and the qualifications of many of the young people represents a basis for discontent.

A positive programme for full employment

A positive programme for improving employment opportunities in the inner city areas is urgent.

1. The government's industrial development certificate powers should be applied so as to benefit selected areas. At the present time they are applied to benefit whole regions of the country—the north-west, the north-east, Scotland and Wales. There are districts in Birmingham and London in which unemployment is so high that it is imperative to direct more industrial and commercial activity to them. Selected districts of our major cities should, like the regions of high unemployment, be designated into regions where industrial development certificates will no longer be required.

2. The government's job creation programme should concentrate on the inner city areas with high unemployment as well as the regions of high unemployment.

3. The effects on job opportunities should become a far more dominant factor in decisions about redevelopment. In far too many parts of our major cities reconstruction programmes have meant the elimination of many small businesses and their replacement with housing, educational and recreational facilities which provide no work for the people concerned.

4. In looking at future land designation for planning purposes and in the allocation of land which central or local government already has in its ownership, the provision of space for commercial and industrial activities should be an important consideration.

5. Small business advisory services should be developed in

inner city areas with high unemployment. As Secretary of
State for Trade and Industry I instituted such a programme
when I realised how many of the small firms which contribute
so much to our employment and export prospects did not
have available to them the same range of information and
knowledge that the larger firms naturally possessed. They
were not as aware as the larger firms of the availability of
different forms of government aid and government grants.
Nor were they aware of the range of government export
services. They were ignorant of some important and up-to-
date methods of marketing. The provision of an advisory
service to small firms and small industries is highly cost-
effective: it is relatively cheap to run and the benefits of the
expansion of these small businesses more than compensate
for any public expenditure involved.

6. We should take advantage of unemployment in the
construction industry to transform the built environment of
our inner cities. When in 1971 I was faced with rising unemployment in the construction industry, I persuaded the then
Conservative government that it was an absurdity when there
was so much to be done that these men should be idle and
drawing unemployment or supplementary benefit. I increased
to 75 per cent the improvement grants for modernising older
houses and saw to it that the grants for the clearance of
derelict land and slag heaps were increased. The unique
scheme of 'Operation Eyesore' was started, whereby any
local authority that had a dirty building, a derelict site it
wished to landscape, or indeed any other eyesore, could
obtain a substantial grant to remove it. This was given on
condition that the work was completed within two years—the
two years in which there would otherwise have been high
unemployment in the construction industry.

7. We should substantially improve training facilities within
the areas of high unemployment in our inner cities.

8. We must see that in these areas the schools and other
educational facilities place a far greater emphasis on preparing
people for the work opportunities that are likely to exist.

9. We must provide better schools. If we are to revive these

areas, less crime and better schools are the best way to bring back the future leaders, the future managers, and the middle classes in general to these localities. Such people will not live in areas of high crime and bad schools. Frequently the areas with the worst housing also have the worst schools. A Ministry of Education inquiry showed that whereas over the whole country 40 per cent of school buildings tended to be inadequate the corresponding figure for areas of bad housing was nearly 80 per cent. The EPA (Educational Priority Area) report on primary schools showed that in the London project area 25 per cent of children change schools during the school year. The teaching staff in urban stress areas also shows a high turnover rate and only a small proportion of teachers have more than five years' experience. A large majority of teachers in these schools come from middle-class or white-collar backgrounds and live outside the areas where they teach. Attainment tests suggest that there are many more lower-attaining children in the urban stress areas than elsewhere, while a high proportion of children have serious linguistic difficulties. The problems caused by past immigration will be with the schools for a long time. What is essential is to provide a more extensive programme of English-teaching for immigrant children. The social problems created by immigrants' inability to communicate with the rest of the community are self-evident. If this prevents them getting jobs it will only intensify the cycle of deprivation.

10. We must organise local government finance in such a way that the declining inner city areas are not the areas where local taxation is at its peak. One of the disasters of the United States has been that high local taxation in the inner cities has pushed out industry and commerce and the more prosperous people. Inner city areas have to meet the high costs that follow from poverty and bad housing, which means that the amount of tax they have to raise per head of the population is very much higher than elsewhere. In these areas the child population is normally much higher, which means that they also have more schoolchildren to support. As industrial firms and the more prosperous families move away, they deprive the areas of major sources of revenue and so add a still greater burden to the already impoverished people that

remain. It is vital that whatever system of local government finance is adopted it is one that prevents this scenario.

11. Crime-prevention must be increased in these areas. The relationship between crime and high unemployment must be recognised. The two are very closely interlinked. In areas of high crime, job opportunities decline swiftly; in areas of high unemployment, crime increases swiftly. There could not be a more vicious circle. It is vital therefore not only that crime prevention is increased in such areas but also that jobs are provided so that the young do not turn to crime, as they always have done in areas of unemployment. In inner city areas three times as many major crimes are committed as in other parts of the cities. But even this is not a true index of the realities of crime in those areas, for the statistics of crime tend to be the statistics of arrests. For much of the petty crime in these districts there are no arrests. There is a mass of vandalism—to public housing and to commercial premises— which is seldom detected and for which there are few arrests but which does immense damage and harm to the prospects of the locality itself. In New York crime is so bad that there are many localities into which the police hardly go. It is vital, if our inner city areas continue to decline, that we do not create no-go areas.

Housing—the vital element

The Lambeth inner city report shows that after ten years of London local government reorganisation a clear and agreed set of planning and housing policies has yet to appear. But during those ten years the pattern of London's problems has changed, and the fear of an over-expanding population has been transformed into concern at a decline in population, a decline that leaves in its wake poverty, homelessness, and bad housing.

It is just this type of problem that London and increasingly many of our other urban areas are going to have to meet, and it demands a total new approach to housing. For one thing we need housing schemes that depend far less on management services. The way such services in, for example, many of the multi-storey flat developments of London have failed to maintain decent standards is indicative of the need to mobilise the family itself to provide its own services, rather than to depend upon others to maintain housing standards.

Housing policy in future should concentrate much more on variety. The appalling conformity of British council housing is but a trailer for what George Orwell's 1984 would be like. Inner city housing should concentrate on small schemes on small sites and avoid the mistakes of the large redevelopment schemes of the 1950s and 1960s. The decline in the population of our inner city areas will provide space— space previously not available. It must be sensibly used, to encourage the middle-class professional worker to return to the inner city, and to provide better cultural and recreational facilities.

So long as public housing continues, the terrible mistake of concentrating the poorer families in the worst estates must be avoided. There is plenty of evidence that local authorities have given immigrants and poor workers the worst of the available public housing. The families with rent arrears tend to be concentrated together. Tenants are charged lower rents for houses in certain estates which are sub-standard, so existing tenants in such estates find themselves surrounded by the rougher and poorer families, and are desperate to move. It may well be that there is a desire for the concentration of ethnic groups on the part of the members of the groups themselves, but it should be a voluntary choice and not a choice made for them.

Tax credits essential

An analysis of who the deprived are, in terms of both housing and income, will show that primarily they are families with three children or more, families with only one parent, families with teenage parents who had children at a young age before their incomes were sufficient to support them, immigrant families and the old and the handicapped, who share the problems of lack of mobility. In the inner cities there is a concentration of all these categories. There is no way to remove the deprivation suffered by them in a civilised way other than by turning to the tax credit scheme.

There is a failure on the part of deprived people to make use of those agencies and services that can help them with some of their problems. They do not know where to go. When they actually attempt to use the services that are available they often find them complicated and beyond comprehension. The various departments of local authorities offer a range of social services but people often have to go to one building to discuss one benefit and to another building sometimes many miles away for another benefit. There is a desperate need to establish one community service centre in these inner city areas of multi-deprivation.

There should be created, if possible, multi-service teams so that the whole range of benefits and facilities is available to the individual when he inquiries at the joint community service centre. There is also a need to establish a much more positive link with the deprived. It should be possible after appropriate surveys have been carried out to organise localised information channels whereby, through voluntary help, important information about new benefits and new services can quickly be communicated to those who need help.

Management for the designated districts

We must move to a new concept of district management, applicable to those inner city areas designated by the Department of the Environment as areas urgently in need of action as a result of their multi-deprivation. The designation of these districts would be agreed with the local authorities, as would the duration of the programmes necessary to tackle effectively the problems involved. The first task would be to identify the problems, and skilled teams would be recruited quickly to assess accurately the housing, educational, social and job-creation problems of the districts. There would then be an agreement as to the programmes required to tackle these problems and an order of priorities would be worked out. From that point onwards the new area management executive would be responsible for implementing the various schemes involved and for producing an annual progress report. In some districts the programme would last five years and in others it would be for a long period. The rate support grant mechanism could be used to see that resources were largely directed to these districts so that they received the correct priority in expenditure.

The urgent choice

The problem of our inner cities is caused by their concentration of people living on the economic and social margins of society. This concentration is increasing. The economic and social conditions are deteriorating. The problem of the inner city is the most serious social problem facing British government. Urgent action is needed if the problem is not to become as intractable as it has in the United States.

The cost of failure to solve the problems of our cities will be paid in lives of misery for many of the inhabitants. The reward of well thought out, dynamic policies could be cities of beauty and opportunity where men and women can decide for themselves how they will work, live and enjoy their leisure.

This is a reward of such magnitude that it should command the highest priority in any political party.

2

A Labour View

Alex Lyon

The problems of the inner cities are now self-evident throughout the world. In particular, the United States experience has
generated a mountain of literature on the subject. It is
surprising therefore that British political parties have taken so
long to react to the challenge—but most surprising that the
Labour Party neglected the issue for so long.

The hard core of the Labour vote lies in the inner city.
Depopulation has put some seats at risk—so that electoral
considerations alone should have provided a political response.
But the inner city is also a microcosm of socialist analysis and
interventionist remedy. The demands of the market have
undermined the social and industrial structures of these
communities and only initiatives by the government and local
authority can revive them. It ought to be the sort of problem
which Labour politicians seize on avidly.

Urban programme

Alas, little was done until 1968 and then only by accident.
Enoch Powell made his 'rivers of blood' speech and Harold
Wilson rushed in with condemnation and a promise of
government help to assist the immigrant groups to adjust to
their new environment. But when the legislation was
introduced in the Local Government Grants (Social Needs)
Act 1969 the Home Secretary, Jim Callaghan, and his Minister

of State, Merlyn Rees, were careful to stress that grants would not be limited to black projects but would be available for any kind of urban deprivation. Thus was the urban programme born.

In fact it was never more than a 'lucky bag' programme. At its peak it had £20 million per year, but since projects were usually funded for five years it meant that there was only about £4 million new money annually. Initially proposals were considered only from local authorities but in 1972 the Conservatives began to entertain proposals from voluntary bodies if they were approved by the local authority. By 1976 about 20 per cent of the projects were voluntary.

Nevertheless, the local authority had to provide 25 per cent of the cost and was responsible for indicating its own order of preference. The Home Office, as the sponsoring department, had then to choose its own priority from a list which was usually four or five times as great as the money available.

Inevitably the selection was haphazard. Two junior officials made the preliminary selection and their choice was altered only if senior officials or ministers had other personal preferences. There was no co-ordinated set of principles on which the selection was made. If the education budget had to be cut, the Home Office might yield to an overture from Education to provide more playgroups. In 1975, when we wanted to use the £2 million deducted from aid to Uganda, as a minister in the Department I was able to get help for a number of black self-help projects.

The result was too little, spread unevenly in ways which had little effect on adjusting the inequalities of the inner city. Nevertheless, the projects illustrated some of the needs not provided for by existing local authority programmes. The urban aid allocation was also immensely popular with voluntary organisation which found it a useful vehicle for funding their pet projects. There is a need for this kind of government pump-priming but it should not be confused with a strategy for reviving the inner city.

Community Development Projects

In 1969 Jim Callaghan, largely at the instance of the best civil servant the Home Office has produced in the last 15 years, announced a series of inner city projects. The objective was to plant a group of community workers in a declining area to stimulate the local people to use existing services to better advantage. The projects had no money to tackle urban poverty. Their expenses were paid by government and local authority and their research was co-ordinated by a national team. The ultimate object was to point the way to more coherent national policies, but in this the experiment was a dismal failure.

The community workers soon learnt that radical political initiatives were required but the government—and still less the local authorities—was unwilling to take the necessary measures. By 1974 the Home Office was totally disillusioned with them and was happy to wind up the remaining projects in 1976. Their major contribution to thinking had been to destroy the concept of small area assistance except for certain kinds of main-line programme like the housing areas.

Inner area studies

The Department of the Environment has always distrusted the Home Office involvement in inner area policy. In 1972 Peter Walker commissioned three studies in Liverpool, Lambeth and Brimingham to establish the causes of inner city deprivation. These studies reported in 1977 and profoundly affected the development of the inner city policy.

Urban deprivation unit

Meanwhile Robert Carr at the Home Office had established a small policy unit on urban deprivation policy with a team of civil servants and outside experts. It toiled for four years and produced very little. The trouble was that Labour ministers at the Home Office accepted too readily Treasury protestations that there was no money available. So whilst Barbara Castle succeeded in winning hundreds of millions for social security, the Home Office attracted only a pittance for inner city poverty.

The unit spent most of its time trying to develop a planning technique for establishing which areas of urban deprivation should obtain greater resources. This came to be known as the Comprehensive Community Programme. Initially it was concerned with only small neighbourhoods but the inadequacy of that approach led to proposals to monitor deprivation over a whole local authority area. A number of pilot projects were to be tested but in the end only one at Gateshead was started.

The White Paper

All this preparatory work had resulted in very little amelioration for the poor in the inner cities but the breakthrough came at a meeting of the Cabinet at Chequers in August 1976. A number of ministers stressed the inadequacy of Labour's response to this problem and as a result of this political pressure and a report from the Burns Committee of Civil servants, a new committee of ministers chaired by Peter Shore was established. The writing was on the wall for the Home Office.

The committee's report led directly to the major change of policy announced in April 1977, followed by the White Paper *Policy for the Inner Cities* in June 1977. Responsibility for the urban programme was transferred to the Department of the Environment. Resources were increased to £125 million in England and Wales and £20 million in Scotland. New partnerships were to be established between the government and seven local authorities which would get the bulk of the money. In addition a number of 'programme districts' qualified for special allocation of urban programme money. The government had at last made a meaningful response to the problem.

Criticism

But it is no more than an initial and very inadequate response. The White Paper tries to identify the nature of the problem but the real difficulty is that no one has been able to isolate the common causes of urban deprivation. Economic decline, physical decay and social disadvantage are no more than useful headings which are not common to all areas of deprivation. Some areas have lost population but some are still overcrowded. Some have aging housing and derelict land but others are much less unattractive. The incidence of unemployment in some of the partnership areas is much lower than in many other districts.

We simply do not know the nature of the problem because we do not have sufficient information. The only comprehensive statistics which are available are in the census and unemployment returns. The census does not measure all indicators of poverty but it helps on housing amenities, space and tenure as well as unemployment and labour market activity rates.

Sally Holtermann at the Department of the Environment analysed the 1971 statistics and concluded that the worst areas existed in conurbations, particularly Clydeside, but that it was difficult to isolate particular areas as outstandingly bad. Even with severe overcrowding, which is an indicator showing one of the highest levels of concentration, priority area treatment would have to be given to 15 per cent of the areas to bring in 61 per cent of all households with this type of deprivation.

By grouping those areas with the highest number of census indicators, it is possible to compile a list of worst areas with Glasgow at the top followed by Islington, Bradford and Salford. Although Glasgow is high on the list of many indicators, they are concentrated on a limited number of enumeration districts whereas the inner London districts take precedence in a wider spread of deprivation. But the metropolitan district of Knowsley is unique in its combination of overcrowding, unemployment and proportion of lower paid, despite the fact that most of its housing stock is very good.

Clearly there is no easy test of a deprived area. The Burns Committee made a selection of areas but emphasised that the list rested on 'judgement as well as analysis and there are important qualifications about the statistical method

involved'. It recommended that ministers should not name
the areas but the White Paper rejected the advice and decided
to concentrate resources on a few partnerships and designated
districts. The first seven were Liverpool, Birmingham, Man-
chester/Salford, Lambeth, London Docklands, Newcastle/
Gateshead and Hackney/Islington.

The means adopted to help the partnerships was in line
with the Burns Committee recommendations. There would
be no new institutional arrangement like an inner city agency
and no special fund save that the urban programme would be
increased. The partnership committees would decide how
best to use the resources available from main-line programmes
with the additions that new urban aid would bring. In the
first three years Liverpool, Manchester and Birmingham were
expected to get £30 million each whereas the London Docklands would get £45 million and Lambeth £15 million.

The programme districts chosen were North and South
Tyneside, Sunderland, Middlesborough, Bolton, Oldham,
Wirral, Bradford, Hull, Leeds, Sheffield, Wolverhampton,
Leicester, Nottingham and Hammersmith. The Burns Committee had not included any Yorkshire district in its list but
political pressure had caused a revaluation. Only £25 million
was allocated to these districts from the urban programme
from 1979 onwards and there is no central government
involvement in their planning strategy.

In addition, a number of areas have been designated to use
the special powers given by the Inner Urban Areas Act to
attract more industry. In addition to the partnership areas
and programme districts, the local authorities are Hartlepool,
Blackburn, Rochdale, Sefton, St Helens, Ealing, Wandsworth,
Wigan, Barnsley, Doncaster, Rotherham, Sandwell, Brent and
Haringey.

The powers are a useful addition to the weapons available
to a local authority to reverse a declining trend but their
effectiveness will depend on the level of resources available.
The measure of this can be seen by comparing the allocation
to Liverpool of £10 million per year against the annual
budget of £131 million. The Burns Committee estimated that
Liverpool would need to spend £11.5 million to make a
discernible difference to the level of general public main-

tenance of the parks and highways. To change the environment
would cost a great deal more than the government has
promised.

The inner cities policy is therefore only a beginning. The
selection is arbitrary. Bradford, which has 11 per cent of its
population living in multi-deprivation, is the third largest
area of deprivation in the country but it is not one of the
partnerships. Newham, which is part of the Docklands
partnership, has only 2.6 per cent of its population living in
the same kind of deprivation. Brighton and Hove have 3 per
cent of their population with the worst overcrowding,
housing amenities and male unemployment but will never
figure in one of these *ad hoc* lists.

Peter Shore is well aware of this inconsistency but argues
that so long as there is so little money, it cannot be spread
too thinly. Of course the urban aid allocation is not the only
way in which the partnership areas will be helped. The rate
support grant is gradually being altered to give more resources
to the cities. The partnerships will now figure largely in any
new allocation of resources, as they did when the Chancellor
made extra money available to the construction industry in
1977. But the fact remains that, by the enormity of the
problems facing the inner cities, the present allocation of
resources is inadequate.

Many Community Development Project workers would go
further and argue that resources alone are not the answer.
What is required is a fundamental change in economic and
political policies so that inequality in our society can be
eliminated. They point out that Liverpool has already had
considerable government help but the downward economic
spiral continues. The immediate response to that claim is
that even the total allocation of resources to Liverpool in
the last 15 years is small by comparison with its needs. But
that may be saying the same thing.

A further step

First, we must find a more coherent way of identifying
areas of greatest poverty. The census indicators do not

measure the quality of education and social service needs, nor
the level of family income. They have little to say about the
standard of the public environment in parks, leisure activities
and highways. We need a set of indicators which encompasses
all aspects of deprivation and which sets a common standard
for every area in the country.

The new housing investment programmes are an attempt
by the Department of the Environment to get local authorities
to establish common criteria of housing need so that resources
can be distributed more rationally. That initiative needs
broadening to cover all aspects of poverty.

The comprehensive community programme, on which the
ill-fated urban deprivation unit was working, still offers the
best hope of a more coherent policy. In essence it comprises
an annual revaluation of the forms and incidence of deprivation in an area based on all statistical information together
with the judgement of officials and councillors. It would
deal with employment, housing, education, health and
personal social services, community facilities and the environment as well as the special needs of groups like the elderly or
disabled. It must deal with the special problems of minority
groups. It must consider the existing policies to deal with this
deprivation. It should also produce an itemised and costed
programme for dealing with the deficiencies which have been
indicated.

It will then be for government to will the resources to
meet this need and to adjust its spending budget accordingly.
All local authorities will take part and will be entitled to
assert a claim to some share of the resources available. If
Brighton and Hove can establish a claim for its impoverished,
it is as entitled to help as any other area.

The needs which will be encompassed in the programme
are all those required to lift the standard and quality of life
of the most deprived in our society. No group should be
omitted. The present policy makes no provision for the
special needs of recent immigrants where their needs are
common. The response should be common but people with
cultural difficulties like language need special provision which
ought to be part of the programme.

The government ran away from this challenge. Paragraph

18 of the White Paper blandly acknowledges that ethnic minority groups have settled in some of the inner areas but points out that they have not settled exclusively in the worst areas. 'Inner area problems and racial problems are by no means co-terminous therefore.' That sentence is both cynical and misleading. 81 per cent of New Commonwealth immigrants live in the worst 15 per cent of the areas of deprivation. No census indicator establishes such a high incidence of spatial concentration. If the White Paper had gone on to say that not all the worst housing or the worst unemployment or the worst depopulation existed in the major inner cities it would have been more true. We need to recognise that a comprehensive poverty programme must include the blacks.

The real challenge

That is what we need—a comprehensive poverty programme. We shall not conquer the problems of urban decay by a few improvement schemes and a band of community workers. We need to re-gear the order of priorities of modern government. All main-line programmes have to be redistributive of resources. Socialism is about equality but we have long transcended the view that equality is solely about progressive direct taxation. Nor is it to be achieved only by a greater level of public ownership of industry. More and more the standard of life of our people depends on the extent to which they share in public spending. Everyone participates to some extent, even if it is only on the roads used by the Rolls Royce. Those on supplementary benefit are totally dependent on public spending. But the better-off middle classes have actually done better out of public education and health services than many with lower incomes.

The new comprehensive poverty approach must be a recognition that we cannot cure that inequality only by more generous financial benefits but also by physically altering the environment in which the poor live. A Labour inner city programme must move gradually, but quickly and effectively, to making the whole of our economic, social and political policies into a coherent redistribution of wealth and power in our society.

3

A Marxist View

Bob Davis and Judy Green

Regionalism and urbanism: some aspects of continuity and contradiction

Britain in the 1970s is experiencing a severe economic crisis of worldwide dimensions. The state has reacted to this crisis by depressing working-class living standards, cutting public expenditure and promoting a large-scale restructuring of British capital. The same period has seen an upsurge of ideas about 'inner cities', 'areas of deprivation', and a variety of other such concepts which have in common the fact that they define problems in *spatial* rather than *socio-economic* terms. These two occurrences are not unconnected.

It has long been the state's practice to confuse the causes and symptoms of the problems thrown up by the uneven development of capitalism. Ideas are promoted which explain social and economic problems in terms of the peculiar characteristics of particular areas and of the people who live in those areas, rather than in terms of the structural arrangements which produce both these characteristics and the related problems. The poor are seen to create their own poverty.[1]

The Costs of Industrial Change, a report produced by the National Community Development Project (CDP) in 1977,[2] described how the official analyses and approaches to the problem of uneven development have remained basically unchanged in form for half a century. The interwar crisis of capitalism gave rise to an account of economic problems in terms of 'distressed areas' or 'regions'. The current crisis has produced a view of urban problems, particularly related to so-called 'inner cities'.[3] We would like here to develop further the parallels between the first interpretation, which we characterise as 'regionalism', and the later 'urbanism'. Their significance lies in the fact that they are used to legitimate particular forms of state intervention in the process of uneven development. What they have in common lies not simply in the manner of the intervention and its stated intention, but also in the potential alternative strategies which they exclude or repress. They are all capitalist interventions by the capitalist state on behalf of capital. The alternatives they repress are socialist ones.

Some examples from Tyneside

In 1934 Capt D. E. Wallace, the Special Areas Commissioner for Durham and Tyneside and a Conservative MP, reluctantly concluded that:

> the chronic unemployment problems could not be solved without large scale commitment of government money for the building of new industries.[4]

Thus began over forty years of state intervention in the regions—involving the establishment of trading estates, the building of advance factories, and a range of subsidies—designed to attract private investment and thereby create new jobs and iron out inter-regional disparities in unemployment and prosperity.[5] Much of the content of the regional package has been promoted by, or drawn support from, agencies within the North-east claiming to represent the 'region'—such as the North of England Development Council (NEDC) of today, on which sit local councillors, trades unionists and employers. Local authorities have actively involved themselves in such issues for many years, especially through their representation on these regional bodies.

Prior to the Second World War, they participated in

various sub-regional development boards as well as a regional (North-east) Development Board, which was founded in 1935 and disbanded when the war broke out. They also engaged in their own publicity. For instance, in the 1930s Tynemouth County Borough Council was a member of the Tyneside Industrial Development Board, the function of which was to advertise the special qualities the Tyneside area had to offer— amongst which were 'an abundance of labour, skilled and unskilled, and no scarcity of girl or women workers'.[6] The key word from the 1930s (and one of great significance right up to the present) was *diversification* away from the so-called 'traditional industries' (shipbuilding and shiprepair, heavy engineering, coal and steel) and into a whole range of new manufacturing industries. This involved attracting both new entrepreneurs and new plant, and 'outstanding inducements' were offered.[7]

The Tyneside Industrial Development Board counted among these not only 'abundant supplies of labour available for new and developing industries' but also good industrial relations. Favourable finance from the Special Areas Reconstruction Association and the Nuffield Trust was also available. Tynemouth County Borough Council itself claimed that the area offered excellent facilities for any industry:

> within the last few years, consequent upon the encouragement of a practical kind from the Commissioner for Special Areas . . . a 'definite crusade' has been entered upon for the development of new industries in the municipality. The Corporation is . . . authorised to offer practical help to new factories and workshops . . . [and] has shown enterprise and built one new factory on its own Trading Estate for the development of a virile local firm.[8]

After the war, the efforts of individual local authorities and their sub-regional development boards became better articulated at the regional level through such bodies as the North East Development Association (NEDA), the precursor of today's NEDC. Significantly, it was a very influential grouping of regional industrialists called the Northern Industrial Group (NIG) which spawned the apparently democratic and representative NEDA. NIG was formed in

1943, in anticipation of peacetime, with the stated aim of stabilising the basic industries whilst simultaneously diversifying so as to create full employment.[9] In setting up NEDA after the war, NIG not only managed to engineer a widespread consensus about what needed to be done, but its initial package of proposals for regional development laid the basis for nearly all subsequent regional development packages. These included:

> the clearance of dereliction and building of executive housing to attract industrialists: government assistance for new factory building: the rationalization of existing centres of population: the construction of trading estates: slum clearance linked to industrial development.[10]

In brief this meant the planning of the necessary 'infrastructure' (financed by the state) to enable fresh capital accumulation to begin. Then, and since then, all the incentives offered under the almost standardised regional package have been, of course, incentives to capitalists. As *The Costs of Industrial Change* put it:

> Governments of whatever political line have relied on restructuring the environment for industry to operate in, building modern advance factories here, new roads there, holding out grants and subsidies all round—hoping to tempt industrialists down the right path by a variety of inducements, rather than seriously trying to control economic development.[11]

It would be a mistake to see regional policy as a successful government 'intervention' in industry. Capitalism has developed in the north—as elsewhere—unevenly; historically there have been two main phases of industrial development in the area and, as we argue later, it seems that a third phase is now in progress. The area 'traditional' industries were once at the forefront of industrial growth in Britain—and, indeed, in the world. Their long-term decline has continued through the post-war years, causing the loss of as many jobs as were actually created as a result of private investment in 'new' industries in the northern region during the most active period of regional policy.

The apparent success of regional policy in the 1950s and 1960s occurred during an era of expanding world markets and a prolonged domestic consumer boom. Government policies were only following capital's needs for resources, including labour. The northern region was softened up by massive state investment in infrastructure. But the new private industries were not directed towards the existing centres of industry where the working classes were concentrated: the region itself had to be restructured in order to fit the requirements of capital, and the state's role here was to facilitate the creation of new centres of industry and population. Far from bringing 'work to the workers', as regional policy was popularly sold, in reality it reshaped the region to suit capital.

The policy effectively met the needs of capital development at that period, and until recently many big national and multinational companies set up operations in the north-east— part of the process of the internationalisation of productive capacity that was occurring at this time.[12] These companies were after cheap labour and a base for their Euorpean operations. They got both; many of the new jobs created were, in fact, jobs for underorganised and lower-paid women workers.[13] State policies channelled capital towards these resource pools. But the policy of 'diversification', relying on the establishment of a new generation of private industry to provide a lasting solution to the problems created by the loss of jobs from existing industries, contained the seeds of its own subsequent failure. This has become evident recently as the 'new' industries have begun to restructure.

The crisis of capitalism

Inherent in the system of capitalism are periodic crises of accumulation produced by the general tendency of the rate of profit to fall.[14] The crisis of the 1970s is particularly severe. During such crises capital makes efforts to restructure itself, to find a way out of crisis and to restore the conditions conducive to further periods of capital accumulation. These efforts include greater investment in plant and machinery, rather than in labour, so as to increase productivity; though this is a continual process under capitalism it is heightened at such times. In addition, capital becomes more concentrated and centralised, through rationalisations, mergers and take-overs. Individual capitalists and firms disinvest from industries where the prospects of accumulation are poor and switch into sounder investments. Ever more workers are thrown on the scrap heap.

The North-east has felt the full effects of this present crisis. Mobile capital is in scarce supply, disinvestment from the older industries continues, whilst restructuring in industries like telecommunications, food and clothing has meant the closure of many plants and drastic rationalisations in those remaining, with massive redundancies.[15] Many parts of Tyneside—once housing mainstream productive industries— are becoming reservations for the subsidiaries of multinationals and their distribution depots, and the more peripheral sectors of the British economy. Unemployment continues to grow and will continue to do so as the combined effects of the economic crisis, of technological innovation, and of the locational strategies of the big business league of firms begin to bite even harder.

Regionalism is now in retreat. It no longer fits in with capital's current need to restructure. The state—being a capitalist state—falls into line: it will not and cannot stand in the way of big capital's withdrawal from 'the regions'. In fact, it actively assists the restructuring. The Labour government's 'industrial strategy' is attempting to make British capitalism more profitable and efficient by encouraging rationalisation and increased investment in plant and machinery, and greater degrees of exploitation by the multinationals.

In launching a programme of selective assistance to different industrial sectors, Eric Varley, Secretary of State for Industry, and Chancellor of the Exchequer Denis Healey talked of 'sustaining a private sector of industry which is vigorous, alert, responsible and profitable'.[16] The overall programme for Bitish industry would be co-ordinated by the (Tory-created) National Economic Development Council

(NEDC), *the* crucial vehicle for the new tripartite state capitalist planning. NEDC would be the forum at which 'a new industrial policy [would be] agreed between government, both sides of industry, and the financial community'.[17] Thus nationalisations, the National Enterprise Board, planning agreements, industrial democracy—all reforms promised by Labour, indeed, at the heart of its reforming programme of 1973—became subsumed under the suffocating tripartism of the NEDC.[18] Through this, the state is aiming explicitly to put capitalism back on its feet again.

Its strategy is to promote a large-scale restructuring of British capital—at home and abroad—in order to make it more internationally competitive and profitable. This is backed up by a mix of policies designed to shift the distribution of national income in favour of profits, including depressing wages and cutting public expenditure (the 'social wage') and public sector employment.

It is widely recognised that the government's industrial strategy will mean fewer jobs in the mainstream of manufacturing industry. The Northern Region Strategy Team predicted the further decline of manufacturing employment in the north, arguing that 'this trend will be reinforced the greater the success of the Government's industrial strategy'.[19]

But the withdrawal of big capital from the regions, assisted by the big-business-based, highly selective and non-graphical 'industrial strategy', does not mean that the resource pools cannot provide locations for future capital accumulation by other investors. The state's role here is to try to smooth the transition between old capital pulling out and the new coming in, and to try to provide the infrastructure for the successful implantation of the new. In this situation, then, another scenario becomes possible—the internalisation of the Third World, or the Empire, the institutionalisation of poverty, and the creation of a 'relative surplus population' of sufficient size to be a permanent pool of low-wage labour, ever available for increased exploitation by capital's new incarnations. How can the state achieve this transition without too much social disruption?

The 'inner city problem' has now replaced the 'regional problem' as the focus of interest and involvement for government, academics, and a range of voluntary agencies. Initially, official ideas about the 'problem' revolved around housing stress, environmental dereliction, decay and redevelopment. More recently, it is the employment aspect which has been emphasised.

Central government—perhaps belatedly—came to acknowledge the importance of industry and employment. Secretary of the Environment Peter Shore's speech in Manchester in September 1976 appeared to set the scene for the reversal of post-war policies which had encouraged the dispersal of jobs and people from the cities and the concentration of new manufacturing investment in out-of-town industrial estates and New Towns. Future policies had to deal with causes, not symptoms, of decline, and therefore with jobs.

> The opportunity to attract industry back to the inner areas now exists in a way in which it did not a decade or so ago.[20]

But how was industry to be attracted back?

> Part of the [current inner city problem] is due to the forces which have led new private investment [our emphasis] in factories and housing to the growing towns and suburbs rather than in new cities.[21]

So

> I see it as the job of central government first to ensure that all its own policies are consistent with our inner city strategy, and secondly to provide the framework and flexibility for local government to foster confidence in the inner cities so that *private investment* [our emphasis] is promoted.[22]

The debate gathered momentum and a new policy package began to emerge. In February 1977 Shore, in announcing that at least £100 million would go to the inner cities to improve their local economies, stressed the need to preserve existing jobs and encourage the growth of new firms by providing a more suitable context for private industry to flourish: services must be better integrated and the environment improved because 'The flow of private investment, whether for commerce, industry or housing, depends among other things on raising the level of the environment'.[23] Inner city policy was beginning to take on a definite—and rather familiar—form. The actual programme for the inner cities which was put together in 1977 included special 'partnerships' between government and local authorities in selected areas in order to establish 'inner area programmes aimed at keeping and attracting jobs'[24] by means of such measures as creating advance factories and improving the environment. These moves were formalised in June 1977, with the publication of the inner cities White Paper which proposed that local authorities should have new powers to assist industry through loans, grants, and the construction of industrial improvement areas. The problems the White Paper identified were seen as having their roots in economic issues:

> the decline in the economic fortunes of the inner areas often lies at the heart of the problem . . . [there has] not been enough investment in new manufacturing industry to counterbalance . . . job losses.

Local authorites were to be the agents for action—but

> authorities with inner area problems will need to be entrepreneurial in the attraction of industry and commerce.

This involved a special effort towards the private sector. In order to strengthen the economy of inner areas, authorities needed to:

> stimulate investment by the private sector, by firms and by individuals, in industry, in commerce, and in housing. The resources and energies of small and medium size firms are essential if real progress is to be made and the diversity, and vitality, for so long characteristics of inner cities, is to be restored.

The role of the local state is quite clear:

> With the public sector ready to create the opportunities
> and to underpin confidence in the inner areas, the attraction
> of new investment and lending should grow. The aim must
> be to encourage changes in the attitudes of industry and
> financial institutions so that they play their full part.[25]

The urgency of the jobs situation was not lost on the
government. But far from representing a genuine 'intervention', the new inner city policies did not challenge current
trends in the private sector of industry at all—rather they
leant over backwards to accommodate them.

This much is clear from another important document
circulated by Mr Shore in mid-1977.[26] *Local Government
and the Industrial Strategy* stressed the problems of the inner
cities, and many of its measures were designed to deal with
these by retaining and encouraging industrial expansion in
such areas. The basic message of this circular was for local
authorities to switch their priorities to industry, even at the
expense of traditional objectives in housing, transport and
land-use planning. Specifically, the circular suggested that
firms should be given all encouragement to develop, that
development plans should have a large industrial content,
that firms should not be displaced by a clearance if possible,
that small accommodation should be provided for small
firms, that partnerships with private developers should be
entered into for industrial estates, and that flexibility in the
housing market should be encouraged with building for sale
to meet incoming or expanding industry. The industrial
pollution criteria were also relaxed.

The relaxation of controls over the exploitation of the
inner cities was matched in its cynicism by the paltry public
expenditure effort on them. Massive expenditure on the
cities—despite the scale of their problems and despite all the
ballyhoo—just could not be afforded:

> We presently face economic difficulties of a scale unparal-
> leled in our post-war history. The economic situation must
> necessarily dominate and constrain our policies on every

front, and must force us to examine all our priorities and programmes.[27]

I regret to say that there is no extra money available waiting to be earmarked for inner cities—so extra expenditure [will come] from within the totals of public expenditure already set.[28]

So the rate support grant was rejigged, with the counties helping to bale out the cities. Chancellor Healey's special 'inner cities construction fund' (established in his March 1977 budget) itself represented a redirection of cash already cut from general capital programmes.[29] The original £125 million per year Department of the Environment 'programme for the inner cities' announced in April 1977 represented an increase of only £95 million over the old Home Office urban aid programme.

Judy Hillman, writing in the *Guardian*, hit the nail on the head when she described it all as a 'beefed up programme for urban aid'.[30] Official Conservative sources called it a 'modest transfer' involving trivial amounts'.[31] The idea that economy was the order of the day is reinforced by the references in the June 1977 White Paper to the 'waste' involved in abandoning the 'inner cities' because of the 'useful economic life' left in the infrastructure, and the 'waste' in the 'prolonged under-utilisation' of that past investment.[32]

Mr Shore had obviously been listening to the advice of big capital, which seemed to be saying, 'do something but not too much'. The *Financial Times* welcomed the low level of expenditure on the inner cities:

The Government's new approach to the problem of inner city decay, as described by the Secretary of State for the Environment . . . adds up to nothing very much. This is only partly to be regretted, since there has been a very real danger that Mr Shore would persuade the Cabinet to allow him to announce the expenditure of further hundreds of millions of pounds on the impossible task of stemming the outward flow of people from city centres to the greener suburbs.[33]

A later comment added:

> Mr Peter Shore is trying his best to produce a piece of
> paper that will live up to his grandiose plans to revitalise
> the inner cities. Whatever he turns out in the end, after a
> tough argument with the Treasury, will probably not be
> too harmful, since there isn't enough money for real
> damage.[34]

Small businesses—the entrepreneur rides again

Not only was 1977 'the year of the inner city'[35] it was also
the year the Labour government resurrected the small
businessman and made him the new hero of the day.[36] A
variety of new government measures were processed during
1977–8 to help small businessmen, including favourable
treatment in successive budgets. In September 1977 a senior
Cabinet Minister—Harold Lever, Chancellor of the Duchy of
Lancaster—was put in charge of the government's small firms
policy. At the same time, similar strategies were finding
favour among official circles in the North-east. Tyne and
Wear County Council, a pioneer in many ways in the field of
local authority industrial policy, was endeavouring to
establish a Small Companies Finance Board, whilst the
regeneration of home-grown entrepreneurial activity formed
a large component of the recommendations of the Northern
Region Strategy Team's Final Report.[37]

This sudden acclamation of the small businessman as the
saviour of the British economy has to be seen in the context
of the present mass unemployment. Harold Lever argued
that:

> If something is to be done for the pool of a million and a
> half unemployed, then small businesses are one of our best
> hopes. In the last ten years, a million extra people have
> been taken on by public authorities. I cannot see them
> taking up a million in the next decade. Nor can we expect
> much from the nationalised industries who are suffering
> from overmanning. And the larger firms in the private

sector are also likely to be shedding labour with the introduction of new technology. It is vital that we help small businesses to expand.[38]

He also made the link with the inner city clear:

> Only a vigorous and self-confident small business sector can provide this extra push of effort we require in inner city areas . . . we must bring [inner cities] back to life with new and modernised housing, shops, showrooms with craftsmen, workshops and small factories. We must encourage the small businessman to return.[39]

This echoed a point made in the *Financial Times* at an earlier stage, when it had encouraged the government to 'let capital rip' in the inner cities.[40] The restoration of entrepreneurial confidence is seen as being of prime importance by Mr Lever and the government. On a similar theme, another spokesman for capital has stated:

> [to maintain and create job opportunities] inevitably means that private businesses and the employment they provide must be encouraged. This will not merely happen because enabling legislation is enacted, but will be the positive response to improving economic conditions and an assertion by the Government that they believe in the role of business . . . By building better roads, by providing modern services, these inner industrial areas can be made as attractive as out-of-town sites, particularly for small businesses.[41]

Those government assurances have poured forth.

> Small firms have always been vital to our economy, but never more so than now and in the years ahead; and never more so than in deprived and dejected inner city areas.[42]

The measures have also been forthcoming—the March 1978 budget package included tax relief for small companies, an expansion of government services to help them, and an extension of the small firms employment subsidy.

Once again, the state is following the dictates of capital; the parallels with regionalism are very close. The inner city has to be softened up for capital so that capital is able to exploit the resources there more fully.

For some time, it has been clear that, although the large traditional employers have been running down their manufacturing investments in the older urban areas, this does not represent a straightforward withdrawal by capital. Capital has found new uses for the inner city—or, more precisely, for its people and its land.

The inner areas of cities like Newcastle have recently seen a new generation of back-street sweatshops mushroom, attracted by cheap labour and cheap premises left behind by the more mainstream industrial activities. Similarly, large tracts of land have become available as former industrial sites are cleared; relatively cheap to develop, these have been occupied by warehousing and distribution depots, many of them belonging to large corporations which use them to store and distribute products made elsewhere. They usually provide only a few lower-paid jobs. More recently the large multiple retailers have also begun to cast their eyes longingly towards these areas; the inner cities, with their ready labour supply, cheap land and proximity to large population centres, offer ideal locations for the giant hypermarkets these firms are currently developing—and they are actively pressuring the government to allow them access to the inner city areas.[43]

Under the present system, industrial investment will take place only on capital's own terms:

> Only when the inner city becomes at least equally attractive to industrialists and business enterprises as green field suburban sites and state assisted new towns will these [necessary] jobs be created . . . Cheap land, adequate transport, attractive environment, and above all good quality housing, are essential preconditions for the attraction of new industries and skills as well as the regeneration of existing firms.[44]

We have seen how capital and its state have responded to

the crisis of the 1970s, and how the dismantling of the post-war package of regional 'reforms' has accompanied the big-business-based industrial strategy. The flip side of this overall strategy is the rather curious mixture of sweeteners for the bitter pills that local workers, and to some extent planning authorities, have had to swallow. These include a range of compensatory marginal 'reforms'—limited domestic protectionist policies, the inner-city and small business measures we have documented, and the whole 'social and economic programme' being conducted in and around the labour market by the Manpower Services Commission (MSC).[45]

Against a background of acceptance of permanent structural unemployment deriving from the mass shake-outs of labour from the mainstream parts of the British economy, it is clear that these marginal 'reforms' can have only a minor effect on the growth of the army of the unemployed.

But what kind of a social formation are these marginal 'reforms' aimed at producing? If the industrial strategy succeeds on all sides, the big business sector of industry will be vastly expanded in terms of its capital base and its role in the British economy (but not in terms of its workforce) with alongside it an expanded low-wage sector—in many instances doing what the former finds it insufficiently profitable to do. The small firms sector generates lower profits and expenses on cheaper labour; through it, and through the MSC, the state is attempting to formalise, by increasing support and supervision, a 'secondary labour market', a 'low wage periphery'.[46] The state is supported by the big companies in this; it is no coincidence that IBM and ICI are involved in the Urban and Economic Development Group (URBED) in an attempt to discover new entrepreneurs.[47]

There are many instances of the small business doing big business's bidding, being totally controlled by and dependent upon a number of bigger firms. On Tyneside, classic examples come from Newcastle's back-street clothing industry, whose continued expansion contrasts with the recent spate of closures of larger-scale clothing concerns in the region. The output from many small Newcastle sweatshops goes to big retail firms like Mothercare, Littlewoods and C&A. These companies gain the advantage of low-wage production, giving them more competitive prices in the mass market—without the odium of actually directly employing people in decidedly poor conditions. Marks & Spencer likewise exercises complete control over many suppliers on Tyneside; a change of ordering policy can close small factories and render their workforces redundant, without fear of opprobrium.[48]

Small firms are being given the run of the inner city areas that no one else wants. Bigger small companies are even being assisted now by the National Enterprise Board. They are, in many respects, the soft option on which to base a 'policy' for national industrial recovery whilst at the same time letting the untouchable big league firms that dominate the economy do what they want. They are also an easy option for local authorities, since the latter hold no power at all over the bigger firms; they might just be able to influence one or two smaller local firms with a grant here and a relaxation of controls there.

But clearly small firms offer no solution to the unemployment problems of local areas. All the effort directed at the small firm can be wiped out by one closure of a major manufacturer. A policy of encouraging small businesses will not help the workers of North Shields if, as is possible, Smiths Shiprepairers (still privately owned by the Swan Hunter Group) goes down the drain in the dry dock along with 1000 workers' jobs. In spite of this fact the headline in an article sponsored by the local authority in a business magazine claimed in 1977: 'Small business the key to North Tyneside's future'.[49]

But local authorities never learn (or do they?). Unlike Tynemouth, Newcastle City Council has only recently 'discovered' local employment problems. Physical planning concerns have occupied politicians—Labour and Tory alike—in Newcastle for most of the post-war period. Large-scale city centre development, slum clearance and 'infrastructural' works have been the order of the day, aimed at making the city a truly 'regional capital'. Manufacturing industry has been of little concern, not least because the offices, shops and services in the centre were expected to generate sufficient new jobs. The loss of population and jobs—which has been going on for many years—has only recently come to the forefront of concern and policy-making. With much of the city centre development complete, and housing programmes stagnating through lack of cash, Newcastle Council has leapt to the centre of the stage with its 'social policies for the inner city', which have latterly developed a much greater concern with employment-creation. Two years ago a 'stress area' programme was set up, allocating limited amounts of cash to those areas of the city ranking lowest on a variety of indicators.

In the wider world, the 'attack on stress' is generally regarded as a step in the right direction—'progressive Newcastle' yet again. Following hard on the heels of the discovery of 'stress' was the discovery of unemployment. A new sub-committee and a special group of officers—the 'Employment Team'—was set up to package land rapidly for potential industrial developers, give help to local firms, and engage in the age-old game of seducing industrialists northwards. A string of promotional publications has issued forth. *Business Focus*—a quarterly bulletin—'has been created to keep you informed of the opportunities and attractions of Newcastle upon Tyne as a development area'. Ironically, this reproduces most of the old cliches and assumptions that have characterised the regional promotional bodies for decades:

> Our aim is to lift the veil off this thriving corner of the North East and dispel the out of date image which has so long persisted in the eyes of strangers.[50]

Another familiar touch was the assurance to prospective employers that cheap and docile labour was here for the exploiting. As Newcastle's chief executive explains:

> To industrialists, I would say this: Newcastle can offer a pool of skilled labour and an abundance of semi-skilled and unskilled labour. The industrial track record on the union front bears comparison with any other area in Europe.[51]

The implications for the workforces of the inner cities or older industrial areas are that they are being softened up for a fresh round of exploitation—as and when needed. With worse wages and conditions and less security compared to mainstream labour market activities, they suffer all around. In addition, of course, trades unionism and workplace organisation are less well developed in the small business sector; Grunwick is only the best known national example.

To those who think that an extreme analogy is being drawn here, we quote Mr Lever himself, who in a debate in the House of Commons on the impact of the employment protection legislation on small firms said that, although he endorsed the purposes of employment protection laws, he was anxious to ensure that they were achieved 'with the minimum of difficulty for smaller firms'.[52] The interpretation widely given to this was that the government would act to cushion small businesses against the Employment Protection Act and other employment reforms won by the working class—and passed by a Labour government—in the 1970s.

We would suggest that, in the long run, the industrial strategy as a whole is opposed to the interests of the working class. It is designed to usher in a new era of exploitation, not emancipation. The last Labour government was the capitalist state's handmaiden in helping to achieve this. The whole strategy deliberately excluded any socialist alternatives. It did not address itself to the fundamental issues of the ownership and control of the means of production, distribution and exchange.

Just like the earlier regionalism, the inner city strategy serves to divert political activity and attention from the overall operations of the capitalist system towards the particular problems and alleged peculiarities of places and people. Also, like regionalism, a whole fresh range of committees and tripartite consultative bodies serve to enmesh and incorporate Labour leaders—councillors, trade unionists, community groups—into acceptance of the state's definition of the nature of the problem, its proposed solutions and, by extension, its own authority and legitimacy.

There are further parallels with regionalism and its view of the working class, for the inner city perspective has a strong 'blame the victim' element. The analysis of the north-east as a region, for example, became honed down to a fine science;

by the use of statistical indicators of various sorts the picture of the 'region' was compounded into one of an area troubled by an outdated economic base and containing, for instance, a greater proportion of manual workers than the national average, lower average *per capita* income and worse housing. These, of course, were the very things which the state said that regional policies would reform; symptoms and causes are conveniently confused by means of a reified concept of 'region'.

But the parallel can be extended. These kinds of technique and the underlying analysis are applied to notions of under-development in the Third World; the inhabitants of poor countries are not viewed as victims of imperialism, but as being unfortunate enough to live in places with unbalanced industrial structures and backward technologies. Not least, the inhabitants themselves are seen as suffering from a range of psychological inadequacies. The problems of imperialism and capitalism are explained away in terms of peoples and places. The inner city debates have again stressed factors like these, and often the blame for their 'condition' (also analysed by sets of indicators) is thrown back on to the inhabitants.

A kind of 'mass pathology' viewpoint has always been lurking beneath the official analysis; Shore's Manchester speech characterised the inner areas as having disproportionate numbers of unskilled and semiskilled workers, and attributed part of the cause (apart from the declining economy) as *policy* mistakes of dispersal arising from bad population forecasts; so that there were 'common problems . . . arising above all from a declining economic and industrial base . . . in part caused by and in part contributing to a major and unbalanced loss of population over the last 15 years'.[53] The Association of Metropolitan Authorities' document *Cities in Decline* compounded this with its insistence that 'the labour force of these areas has become increasingly composed of those with inherent employment problems (the "secondary labour market")'.[54]

The theme has reappeared regularly ever since. In his speech at the Bristol 'Save Our Cities' conference, Shore alluded to the social considerations lying behind the inner cities initiatives—including crime. And the White Paper reiterated not only the theme of an 'unbalanced' population (skilled workers migrating out, leaving behind a pool of less skilled workers who by implication cannot cope) but also the idea of 'collective deprivation', manifesting itself in a 'pervasive sense of decay and neglect' in some inner areas. It was this which, in fact, provided 'an important argument for tackling inner city deprivation on an area basis and for discriminating in favour of the inner areas in the working out of public policies and programmes'. Their decline needed arresting too, for fear of contamination—'the heart of our cities would suffer as the surrounding inner areas went further downhill'.[55]

But, as we have seen, psychologically inadequate or not, the inhabitants of inner cities are still ripe for exploitation. To this end they are bundled up as 'factors' and sold to investors. In both regionalism and urbanism, labour appears as a passive variable waiting for exploitation, not as people or local workers with rights and powers over the provision of work. Under the rules of capitalist industrial development, those in whose name the policies are undertaken in the first place must await the decision of the capitalist as to whether or not they will even get the chance to be exploited.

There is of course a crucial dimension lacking from this account, which is the class struggle. Restructuring involves— in fact, is part of—the class struggle. There is no inevitability about the outcome. Labour organisations can fight the industrial strategy of the capitalist state. Whether they do, and how they do it, will affect the overall outcome and is not something we can speculate about here. One thing about the reversal of policies towards the small business sector of petty bourgeois capital that is sure is that the conditions for the pursuit of capital accumulation and growth are being recreated for this sector of capital at this moment in time. But that, of course, sows the seeds of its own reversal, as it entails yet another process in the historic conflict between capital and labour.

True to the traditions of bourgeois reformers, the problem is defined not as one intrinsic in capitalism, but as inherent in peoples, as one of social and political order and the integration of the growing underclass into civil society. 'Action' means giving a grant to a voluntary organisation, sponsoring a

community project or perhaps holding a conference; a game
for the new generation of 'exchange professionals' between
the state bureaucracy and the working class. (We have no
wish to exclude ourselves from this kind of criticism.) The
new quasi-professional and the 'volunteer' do play an
important part, because:

> a new and closer form of *collaboration* [our emphasis] is
> required between government and the private sector . . .
> and the community . . . representative organisations . . .
> voluntary bodies, and above all with the people living in
> the inner areas . . . [whose] welfare . . . must be the
> ultimate touchstone for success.[56]

Mr Shore is:

> enormously encouraged . . . [by the] . . . new concern
> about the cities amongst people of all political parties,
> academics, journalists, social workers, industrialists—and of
> course the inhabitants themselves.[57]

Another round of incorporation?

Unlike other contributions to this volume, this piece is not
directly concerned to consider immediate practical policy
measures for particular aspects of the 'inner city problem'.
Rather, it is our intention to demonstrate that, with a
historical perspective, the problem can be seen as nothing
new—though its guise has changed slightly. The overall
problem is deeply political. It is our contention that there
can be no easy technical, administrative or politically neutral
solutions to the major social and economic problems which
underlie, and cause, the 'regional' or the 'inner city' problems.

Solutions are available only at the political level. This
much is clear from the whole debate; the parameters have
been so tightly drawn that even limited left social-democratic
debate about the need to tie in discussion of inner city
programmes with those on public intervention in private
industry in the interests of workers and consumers is ruled
out. The restriction of these parameters is itself a political
act. The result is that policies based on analyses borrowed

from the context of regionalism are transplanted on to the inner cities in a similar attempt to repress the alternatives. Strategies now discredited as unsuccessful in their avowed intentions are mustered fit for the futures of inner city dwellers. The only fit social action for the inner cities is the sabotaging of the current strategy, along with the system that has bred it.

Part 2
Local
Government

4

The Inner City Partnerships: a Critical Assessment

John Tilley

The great inner city initiative, launched by Peter Walker and brought into reality by Peter Shore, is at a critical point in its development. It can either go forward to become a new and distinctive form of public intervention effectively combining for the first time both central and local government, or it can simply be absorbed without trace into the existing bureaucracies.

The inner urban pioneers have reached the end of the beginning, and now they, and the people they represent, have to decide whether the next stage will be as fruitful and exciting as the first one. Peter Walker decided that the inner urban problems had to be studied not only in depth but in connection with each other.

Peter Shore, when he saw the results of those studies, evolved a strategy for putting into practice the lessons which they drew. He inevitably stressed the first visible aspects of his strategy—the partnership committees which by their very existence would sweep away the compartmentalised thinking of government departments and local councils which had always been a hindrance to any concerted approach to inner city problems.

He also stressed the extra funds that would be available for tackling the problems, and he naturally found political relief, in a time of massive cuts in public expenditure, in being able to portray these extra funds as evidence of the Labour government's determination to fight social inequality in spite of the International Monetary Fund.

Those years were a heady period of White Papers, eloquent speeches and high hopes. To say that great expectations were raised is not to criticise the government approach. One of the principal objectives of the inner city policy was to raise the morale of the people living there, to make them feel that they had not been forgotten, that help was at hand. This was not a cynical or electoral ploy. It was a realisation of the fact that renewed self-confidence among the local community was an absolutely vital ingredient of inner city regeneration.

The low morale existed among elected councillors as well as individual citizens. Labour councillors had seen the great 'housing starts' boom of the 1964-70 Labour government transformed into a nightmare of industrialised buildings that were expensive to repair and difficult to let—mainly tower blocks. The Victorian terraced slums had been replaced by new vertical slums. The housing waiting lists had shrunk but not dissappeared, while the transfer lists had grown rapidly. The return of a Labour government in 1974 brought security of tenure for furnished tenants, but even this measure did not stop a growth in the numbers of homeless families.

The new Labour ministers, who rightly refused to copy their predeccessors of the 1960s by using housing starts as a socialist virility symbol began a much more considered policy of trying to influence council building in a way which would provide new housing of lasting worth and attractiveness. Such a policy was, by its very nature, slow to take effect and Labour councils, particularly those in inner cities, began to realise they were not going to get sufficient emergency aid from the government to solve their immediate housing crisis.

In other fields, too, local authorities were finding that the traditional solutions were not working. The 1970 Local Authority Social Services Act, with its mandatory establishment of single social services departments to end the ludicrous overlapping and duplication of the welfare services, could not be faulted in logic but its most obvious effects were to increase the cost of the services, as the sum of the whole was much larger than the sum of the parts, and to identify an ever widening area of demand and need.

Councils were also dimly realising that employment in the inner city was no longer something that could be left to central government and private capital. Even when this realisation had been made and the extent of job loss had been measured it was still hard to know what to do about it. There is no simple way of turning a local authority that has been set up by statute as a body to clean the streets, empty the dustbins and build council houses, into an instrument of economic intervention and public entrepreneurship. Some councils tried to adapt themselves in this way but it was a slow and cumbersome performance and produced more committee resolutions than jobs.

Added to all this was the development that crept up on all councils in the early 1970s—the growth of a network of individuals and organisations who challenged the right of elected members to speak exclusively on behalf their electors. The names were manifold—community action, neighbourhood councils, voluntary bodies and so on—but the effect was the same. The political monopoly of elected councillors was challenged in the press, in the council meetings and in the streets, in a way that took elected members as much by surprise as it did the Town Hall officials.

The genuinely representational nature of these groups differed widely. Some community activists were strong-minded and strong-voiced individuals who were able to get a better hearing because they claimed quite falsely to be speaking for 'the community', but many were and are much more representative. Indeed their democratic base in the inner cities was often wider than that of the local Labour Party which selected the councillors. Genuine or not, they could not be ignored and councils got used to involving, or carefully avoiding, this new vocal group.

Given all this—the despair about housing and social problems, the frustration over employment and the mixture of confusion and embarrassment about community activists— it is hardly surprising that Labour councils reacted with delight when the new Secretary of State for the Environment unfolded a new philosophy which explained away their puzzlement and promised to sweep away the frustrating obstacles. Although Peter Shore may appear to be an unlikely urban Messiah he was welcomed with open arms by many people—councilors and officials alike—because the new gospel seemed to have all the answers. A few years later its great strength appears to be that it dodged, rather than answered, at least some of the questions.

The doubts which have arisen should not be allowed to diminish the validity of many aspects of the new inner city philosophy. Four propositions are central to the philosophy.

1. That greater co-ordination is needed to tackle interlinked problems.
2. That more money is needed to tackle these problems.
3. That the local economy—particularly the number of jobs available—is the key to inner city revival.
4. That a new approach is needed on housing, and the answer is not just more of the same in terms of new building or municipalisation.

The trouble has come with the attempts of central and local government to turn these great new commandments into real policy. The current series of problems about the inner city initiative centres round the doubts which are now being felt about the implementation of these four maxims.

Is the co-ordination of policy effective?

Politicians are often tempted into thinking that a correct choice of label will make the object labelled resemble the description on the label. This may be good sociological theory, but it is bad government. Just because legislation is called the Community Land Act it does not follow that the implementation of that Act will give the community control over the land.

Equally, putting a group of politicians into a room once every three months and calling them a partnership committee does not ensure that they will act in partnership. The very opposite may be the case. The co-ordination aspect of the inner city initiative, of course, covers much more than the partnership committee meetings, which are said to be merely the tip of the iceberg.

The iceberg is the greater degree of co-ordination, co-operation, liaison and so on between officials—civil servants and local government servants. These interchanges take place formally at the officer steering groups which meet monthly and on a day-to-day informal basis as issues arise.

The links have undoubtedly been the major achievement so far of the inner city initiative. The departmental and central-local barriers, which meant that policy was piecemeal and haphazard, have been broken down.

A new dialogue has been established but fears are now being expressed as to whether it is balanced enough in view of the dominance of one partner—the Department of the Environment. This department naturally takes the lead between government departments because the inner city initiative is based in its traditional sphere of responsibility for housing and local government. It takes the lead in the relationship with local government largely because the bulk of the inner city money comes from the taxpayer rather than the ratepayer.

The DoE has widened its powers through the initiative. It now has a major say in the decisions of departments such as employment and industry, which were previously outside the ambit of local government. It has much more power over the programmes and policies of the local authorities in the partnership areas, because it has a right of access and consultation which would not have been entertained before. No partnership council can 'do a Clay Cross'.

There is evidence enough that the partnership is not really equal—that one partner is more equal than the others. A classic example of this is the issue of making the partnership meetings open to the public and the press. Every department that I have consulted, and every local authority involved in the Lambeth partnership, claims to be willing to hold the meetings in public. Only the DoE refuses to agree and forces its ministers to make lame excuses—saying that the partnership committee is not a statutory body but merely a consultation between statutory bodies.

This attitude is disastrous for public relations because the local community quite rightly wants to see and hear partner-

ship committees work in practice. But the great new initiative
that was launched with press conferences and razzmatazz is,
within a few months, being described as merely 'a consultation
between statutory bodies' and no business of mere electors
and ratepayers.

Is the money enough?

The second doubt is financial. The immediate reaction to the
inner city programme was that, in a time of public expenditure
cuts, it was manna from heaven, and those local authorities
which were excluded from the partnership scheme protested
loudly, to mix metaphors, that now that the partnership
boroughs had arrived at the end of the rainbow the crock of
gold was not quite as big as it seemed. Like all money it is
infinitely better than nothing, but the question now is
whether it is enough to do the job of reviving the inner city.

The problem is that if inner city initiative means a new
direction of policy in many areas, then by definition it is
impossible to say what this will cost—except, of course,
more.

The cost of 'reviving the local economy', which is the
glibbest of all the phrases used in promoting the inner city
initiative, is unknown, yet it is the key to the whole operation. No one can imagine for a moment that the inner city
areas can become bottomless pits for public money, poured
in to help a totally helpless community who cannot find
work, will not move, and have no resources of their own.
This usually goes without saying, but it helps to say it,
because it leads on to the next step.

Who creates the jobs?

The third key issue is that the only way a bottom can be put
into the pit is for more people to have jobs, which generates
demand, which maintains incomes, and which provides
another focus for self-help through workplace organisation.

So the authorities in the partnership have a collective responsibility to prepare people for jobs and then provide the jobs. The preparation side of this is a task for education and employment departments—together with the local education authority—and these bodies seem to be tackling the problem well; and they have plenty of money, at least for post-school training. But the cost of providing jobs cannot be quantified or planned as easily as can the cost of training the unemployed workforce to be able to take them.

The regional industrial policy of the last twenty years cannot be used as a yardstick of cost because the regeneration of the inner cities economy will not consist, as so much of regional policy does, of getting very large employers who already have several factories to set their next one up in a particular region. It consists of preserving existing small companies and promoting new ones. This is a much more complex operation and government departments are at the stage of feeling their way into a new sphere of policy.

Unfortunately the greatest danger on the employment aspect of inner city policy is not that government and local authorities are finding that they have signed a blank cheque for industrial development, but rather that even the limited resources available are not being used as they should be. The new gospel of inner city analysis says that lack of jobs is the biggest single problem and the creation of jobs is nearest to a panacea. But the institutional weight of the partnership partners tends to restrict the degree to which this theoretical priority is translated into actual priority. Of the seven ministries involved in the partnership most are mainly service 'spenders' (housing, health, social services, education, transport, etc.) Only industry is concerned with job-creation in its literal sense.

Among the local authorities industrial development is a new and minor responsibility. The officials or committee chairman concerned with it have little clout compared with the directors and chairmen of housing, social services, amenities, or recreation, who have shelves full of schemes that suddenly become vital for the inner city revival. The complete switch-round of policy that should have put industrial development at the top of the agenda has somehow just become the old agenda with economic revival slipped in under 'any other business'.

Where do the houses come from?

The fourth key to a successful inner city philosophy relates to housing. Housing is the one area where local authorities have changed tack. Redevelopment is out. Rehabilitation is in. So far so good. The limited increases in housing investment programmes that have been given to the partnership boroughs have enabled them to get their conversion programmes—that were disrupted and slowed down by the cuts—back on course. But that is all. Private landlordism is on the way out and the 1974 Rent Act reduced to a minimum the numbers of families that would be hurt directly by the process.

If the inner city authorities are to provide decent housing for their inhabitants then they need resources, to be able to municipalise the rented sector at a much faster pace, so that they can house those people—the young, the single and the mobile—who traditionally have depended on the private sector. This costs a lot of money, which is not being provided under the inner city initiative. They also need housing resources—outside their own boundaries, in the form of homes or building land—if they are to make any impact on their massive waiting lists.

The community

However, the most conspicuous failure of the inner city initiative in its first phase has been the inability of ministers to retain the confidence of the 'community groups' who were mentioned earlier. This disillusion was inevitable. Ministers were working against the calendar to get the policy rolling before the government expired. They had to tackle the biggest problem of getting better co-ordination between departments and councils. Those were real constraints.

In the meantime the hopes and expectations of community groups had quite wilfully been raised by politicians at national and local level. For people working at the grassroots in the inner city—struggling day to day themselves with the problems and trying often vainly to persuade those even more deprived than themselves to join in the fight to improve things—to these people the Gospel of the Inner City was almost a glance at the millenium. They expected salvation, and they told their members that help was finally at hand, that the DoE cavalry were just about to come over the hill to their rescue.

Today's community groups do not expect to be given salvation from on high. They want to find it for themselves, or at least to be involved in the decisions on how significant improvements can be made. That has not happened, with the result that there are now three barriers which must be removed before effective co-operation is achieved.

Firstly, the community activists are resentful of their non-involvement. This can only be remedied by adding structured procession consultation on to the partnership committees, so that the groups can be sure of getting their views before the partners. The underwriting of this guarantee must be that the partnership committees meet in public.

Secondly, the community groups' involvements in the inner city programmes are now similar to those of the various council departments—they have simply brought their pet projects off the shelf. These may be more directly relevant to the needs of a local community but they are still piecemeal items.

Thirdly, because of their exclusion so far the community groups have not been able to contribute to the changes of central policy which were the essential ingredient of the inner city programmes.

The inner city initiative is, potentially, the greatest development in social policy since the war. But it must outgrow its central and local government parents and develop a character and strength of its own. The partnership must be between three sections—the government, the local councils and the local people. All three are equally vital.

Only if all the partners are involved can the tough decisions—which have not yet been taken—be faced. The tough decisions must, for example, be that employment has the top priority to the exclusion of everything but housing. And housing cannot succeed unless there is a change in direction.

The three partners must agree on a very few priorities—and put the rest of the possibilities firmly to the back of the queue. Then the government partner must realise, and must finance, the massive costs which are essential for success in these fields.

What the local authority response should be now

The initial response of local authorities in the partnership areas has been a combination of gratitude for having been chosen and deference to the Department of the Environment's ideas of how the initial structures and programmes should be instituted.

The advantages of this have been the speed with which action has been taken, the lack of any major central-local wrangles and the general support that has come from all political parties. On the other hand, the disadvantages have been the failure to think through any major changes in direction of policy, the failure to assess, or even attempt to assess, whether the financial resources are anywhere near sufficient, and the widespread disillusion of public opinion, and particularly of interested community groups.

Now the local authorities should take up the front-running from the Department of the Environment. They are in the key middle position in the partnership—provided they ensure that it is a three-way partnership. If they do that and forge much better links with their own local public opinion then they will be in a much stronger position to force fundamental reviews of policy from the government.

That is their first new role. Without antagonism, and without forgetting the essential contribution of the Department of the Environment in launching the new programme and extracting some money from the Treasury, local authorities have got to demand that government thinks through the unresolved policy issues at the heart of the inner city dilemma. Two examples of the unresolved issues go to the heart of the suggested priorities of employment and housing.

The small firms subsidy pays £20 a week for six months

towards the wages of every new employee taken on through expansion or creation of small manufacturing firms employing fewer than 200 people. This subsidy applied only to the assisted areas until spring 1978, when it was announced that it would be extended, as part of the inner city initiative, to the partnership areas as from July 1978.

This appears to be a breakthrough of recognition that the inner cities are as much in need of government help in encouraging new jobs as are the assisted areas—the traditional development regions—but by July 1978 in the Lambeth partnership area there had not been a single application for this subsidy. Maybe interest will pick up after the starting date.

But maybe not, because although the title of the subsidy may make it sound extremely well suited to the needs of the inner city—where the firms are small—the detail is far less well suited, because the subsidy only applies to manufacturing firms. In Lambeth only 15 per cent of those employed are in manufacturing. In the middle of a national recession the only hope for an expansion of small firms must be in services and distribution—particularly in a place like Lambeth, where the only possible advantage to be exploited is the closeness to central London, where there is a much greater demand for services than there is for manufacturers. The government will have to decide soon whether to bring forward a small firms subsidy that is suited to the needs of the inner city, rather than assuming that any old hand-me-down from regional policy will do.

In housing the issue is housing land. If the inner city local authorities do not have any more housing land, if the previous stratagem of demolishing existing housing to build new cannot be used because it has been shown that it simply produced tower block estates with high child densities, if there is still a long waiting list for housing, and if the new inner policy philosophy says that we must try to ensure that people other than the young and skilled have a chance to move out of the area if they want to—then there must be housing land resources made available outside the local authorities' areas. From the inner city the only direction you can go is to the outer city. Lambeth, for example, must have housing land in outer London if it is to have the slightest opportunity of carrying out the housing policy envisaged in its inner city programme.

Yet the process is going the other way. The outer boroughs and the Greater London Council have stopped building in outer London and they are busy selling off all their existing housing stocks there—the very houses into which the Lambeth families might have been transferred.

The local authorities must impress government that part of its job as the overlord of the inner city programme is to put pressure—and if necessary legislative compulsion—on those authorities outside the partnership areas whose policies are very relevant indeed to the success of the partnership.

At the same time local authorities must build strong links with their own public. This is not just an optional extra, a bit of public relations and good sense electorally. It should be an integral part of the policy. It had to be neglected somewhat until now because of the emphasis on central-local co-ordination.

Satisfactory participation costs money and, more importantly, time—time in the sense of man-hours that councillors and officials have to put in at meetings with the public and time in the sense that these processes delay the completion of programmes and the taking of decisions. If that time and money is given grudgingly and in quantities insufficient to do the job properly then it will be wasted because the interested public will feel that they have been conned, that they have gone through a charade of consultation in which they did not have the time or the information to make a proper response.

Public participation should be carried out fully and properly, or not at all. As 'not at all' is no longer an option, then that leaves 'fully and properly' as the obvious course. This means a steady flow of information by papers and meetings to interested groups and individuals. It means the public having easy access to officials and councillors, both to get further information and to channel back their views.

It also means that there must be a clear procedure for the views of interested groups or individuals to be put to the committee. The committee meeting is the key. Since ministers come to the particular locality only once every three months the committee meeting is the only point at which they can be convinced of the needs and feelings of the area. That is why the partnership meetings must be open to the public and the press.

But public participation in the inner city programme is not just a matter of consulting people about whether they like what the council and the government are going to do and occasionally slipping them a few pounds for their own little pet project. It must mean the involvement of local people in the implementation of the actual policy itself. The energy, determination and intelligence of the people of the inner city are the only resources that have not yet been tapped.

In employment, co-operative workshops; in housing, tenants' associations with power over their estates; in education, the parents' associations; in every local amenity, the involvement of the local users in the management. This is the sort of full participation that is needed.

One of the underlying purposes of the inner city initiative is to rebuild the support systems which a longer-established and more stable community has but which are often lost through the mobility and disruption of inner city living. Rebuilding that sort of community can only be from the bottom upwards by willing co-operation, not by decree.

Finally, and most importantly of all, if local government is to have this added leverage on central government and to involve the people of the area in the great inner city initiative, then it must also set its own house in order.

That means genuine acceptance that the old policies were not enough. When there was money in the 1960s the problem was not tackled. Now that there is less money, even with the inner city extra cash, new policies are needed, particularly on the housing and employment fronts, if any kind of success is to be achieved.

5

The Social Services and the Inner City

Jef Smith

It will be convenient for the purposes of this article to resurrect the inelegant but practical word 'slum'. Already jargon for something very unpleasant when Dickens wrote, it fell into total disrepute once town-planners coupled it with 'clearance', and the stigma of confessing to living in an area judged fit only for demolition naturally made it unpopular with residents. Planners, social workers and others who had to deal with the phenomenon have readily coined a string of euphemisms, to a point at which no one likes the term expect newspaper sub-editors, for whom its brevity represents a neat column-filler. Perhaps it will help in escaping some of its undeniably derogatory overtones, as well as supplying it with a plausible retrospective etymology, to claim at the outset that it is to be understood as an abbreviation for Selected Location of Urban Malaise.

British social administration used to be characterised by a sense of continuity, but the recognition of a major urban problem in the late 1960s has led over the last decade to an unprecedented series of short-term programmes, most of them concentrated on groups of small-area local schemes. Community development projects, comprehensive community projects, inner area studies and partnership areas have each succeeded the other, the last still in an operational phase. (A generic name is needed for these programmes, perhaps Selected Locations of Urban Malaise—Bureaucratically Energetic Responses, which also provides a pronounceable acronym!) The first of these systematic interventions on inner-city deprivation was the Community Development Project, the earliest public papers on which date from 1969. The urban programme had been announced by the Prime Minister in the previous spring as a response to American experience, to a growing recognition of the special social problems of the centres of large towns, and to anxiety about the racial tension in these areas which Enoch Powell had graphically captured in his 'rivers of blood' speech just a fortnight before. The initial impetus for the creation of CDP[1] came from the Children's Development Group, a Home Office working party chaired by Derek Morrell. Morrell's early death left him with an extraordinary, almost mythical, reputation as a visionary and innovator. Among colleagues he is remembered as a remarkably creative civil servant, though Richard Crossman, his minister, was not altogether appreciative of his talents.[2] The initiative on action to tackle the social problems, however, was far from merely personal.

The thinking of the Children's Development Group had developed, significantly, from the work carried out on the Children and Young Persons' Acts of 1963 and 1969, in which the concept of preventive intervention by social workers with families suffering acute and multiple problems had been given legislative form. Central government has no executive powers in the delivery of personal social services, and this absence of direct field involvement—compared with the health and income maintenance services, for example— proves a continued stimulus to ministers and their officials, even if the products of their thinking often owe more to imaginative conceptualisation than to concrete experience.[3] The early waves of thinking on the inner cities came, therefore, from policy-makers concerned with social welfare services, a relationship which has not, unfortunately, been maintained. Indeed, the contacts between, on the one hand, the successive programmes mounted to meet the slum problem and, on the other, the mainstream growth of the personal social services have been intermittent and remain patchy. Why should this be?

The first reason is one applying to any area of local government activity. Local authorities operate only occasionally, and then reluctantly, in concert, valuing for much more of the time the nominal independance with which the British constitution endows them. It is not easy then for local government as a whole to approve policies from which local authorities benefit selectively, as the tension over the annual rate support grant negotiations demonstrates. When the Association of Directors of Social Services set up a working party on deprivation it specified that it would consider both rural and urban poverty,[4] and as areas have been selected for each successive wave of projects, those not chosen have complained, and surely with justice.

Not unnaturally, the local authorities also retain a suspicion that poverty policy represents an attempt by central government to exercise local power. The North American precedent and the battle between federal and states' rights was initially telling if ultimately misleading. More permanent is the paradox that under a system heavily dependent on locally raised revenue, poor areas can only become relatively richer if they are willing to receive positive discrimination in the distribution of central cash. The partnership model is the latest strategy for presenting Whitehall's involvement in Town Hall business in a locally acceptable fashion, for the area committees, in this as in previous ventures, are chaired by government ministers.

The reorganisation of local government in England and Wales fell more or less in the middle of the decade of Britain's poverty programme.[5] That reform—taken with the simultaneous reorganisation of the health service,[6] the very rapid growth in public spending, particularly on the personal social services, which preceded it and the period of sharp retrenchment which has followed—profoundly affected the response of local authorities to the stream of central government initiatives on inner city policies. The social services had, of course, experienced an earlier reorganisation with Seebohm implementation in 1970-1,[7] so that both staff and councillors have experienced a period of such constant structural change that energy has often been lacking for consideration of the content of services.

The integration of health, welfare and child care activities into social services departments remains one of the few thoroughly successful examples of the rationalisation of local authority functions on more corporate lines. Successful policies to tackle inner urban deprivation must necessarily involve a range of local authority departments as well as other services.

Nor does the co-ordination of effort to meet the needs of slums stop at the boundaries of single local authorities. Housing and social services emerged from the 1974 reorganisation as separate tiers of the structure in the greater part of the country, though their convergence in metropolitan districts lessened the problem of joint working in the major conurbations. (The London situation is confused by the continued existence of the GLC Housing Department, a split recently deplored by the Marshall Inquiry.[8]) Education and social services, again with the exception of Inner London, are the responsibility of the same councils, though the traditional and to some extent statutory independence of education committees militates against their full participation in corporate working. The further 'organic' changes proposed by the Labour Party might widen this gulf and have been sharply opposed for that reason.[9] Most significantly of all, health services remain outside the family of local government operations, and despite the coterminosity of local authorities and area health authorities since 1974 (again London excepted) it has required an elaborate and not altogether effective arrangement of joint consultation to achieve combined action.

Perhaps for this reason, the client groups whose needs overlap health and social services—the chronically sick and handicapped, the elderly, the mentally disordered—have attracted less attention in inner city discussion than the children and families for whom local government has a more comprehensive brief. The reports of the inner area studies[10] made frequent reference to the depressing situation of the elderly and disabled in city centres. The elderly have particularly suffered from the decline in public transport and local shopping facilities. Because they are unwilling to move they often experience poor housing conditions and become isolated from more mobile young people. They are especially vulnerable to crime and vandalism. The structure of the inner city partners takes these problems more into account than ever before, and in the distribution of extra resources early use was made of the joint funding arrangements set up and gradually developed by the DHSS over the previous three years.

The client group to whom most attention has been paid in the context of the need for greater collaboration between local authority departments is the under fives. The inadequacy of day-care facilities to meet the demand from working parents, even that of priority groups like lone mothers, has repeatedly been pointed out, by the local authority associations and the government's Think Tank,[11] among others, but the division of responsibility between education departments (nursery education), social service departments (day nurseries and daily minders) and voluntary organisations (most play groups) makes concerted planning extremely complex. The various agencies are separated not merely by their areas of responsibility but also by significantly different ideologies: education limited to activities with a learning content, social services confused about the degree of selectivity to be exercised and torn between a commitment to close family life and the need to raise families' incomes, the voluntary sector deeply committed to parental participation in the management and running of services. Solutions to these problems are not readily to hand but they are receiving urgent consideration; the Lambeth inner city partnership, for example, concluded from an initial study that it should give further consideration to four key issues on pre-school children—the demand for full day-care, the employment needs of women, the special needs of ethnic minority groups, and the position of single-parent families. Hackney Borough Council declared work in relation to children under five as its first social services priority.[12]

Large and poor families, ethnic minorities and teenagers, particularly the disturbed, delinquent and unemployed, have also attracted a good deal of attention. Of course, these groups exist outside as well as within the inner cities and discussion has reflected a wider context—the largely political call for a general family policy, consideration of race relations in all its aspects, and growing concern about disturbed adolescents. For each of these problem areas the importance of the multi-service approach is repeatedly stressed.

The sort of corporate approach to social policy allegedly essential to tackling the problem of the slum, however, has not been helped by the burgeoning professionalism of social work. Social workers have difficulty in expressing their expertise to laymen—their committee members, their clients, their ratepayers—and they are justifiably suspicious of any movement which might dilute their unique contribution as qualified practitioners. The use of volunteers, more particularly the promotion of self-help activities in deprived communities, implicitly challenges a narrow professional definition of the social work task.

Encouraging self-help and self-determination within urban communities has remained a prominent objective of the inner city programme and social work doubts have persisted. The very term 'partnership' is an attempt to express and resolve the tension which undoubtedly exists between the policies of bringing in extra resources to deprived areas and of insisting that communities must participate, if not take the lead, in solving their own problems. 'Local residents', announced the general secretary of the Birmingham Voluntary Service Council, 'are really going to be given the opportunity to understand and to contribute to the problem',[13] but if problems are very complex, if solutions depend on regional or national policies, and if the contribution most required is the resources of which the area is already short, the participation of local residents cannot but be marginal.

The implementation of Seebohm had one very important and largely unexpected by-product—the very rapid growth of research and development sections within the new departments. The Seebohm Committee had carried out little formal research in preparing its own conclusions, but its famous epigram, 'social planning is an illusion without adequate facts; and the adequacy of services mere speculation without evaluation',[14] provided a text for directors of social services seeking an information and investigation capacity within their new structures. Significantly, many of the initially more substantial research sections were in urban authorities—

Coventry, Tower Hamlets, Lambeth, Cheshire—and the creation of the Social Service Research Group built links between the new researchers and town planners, academics and central government.

Nevertheless, the skills required for research in the social services, which have continued to play a major part in the analysis of urban problems, run in many respects counter to the traditions of social work. Social workers are still largely clinicians. Their unit of operation and of recording is the individual or the family, an approach which makes aggregation difficult and which stigmatises even the collection of client statistics as dehumanising. If anything, Seebohm implementation strengthened these tendencies by plunging most social workers into generic caseloads so that their capacity to draw general conclusions about categories of clients was undermined by the very variety of their work and the relatively rare incidence of similar cases in the experience of individual officers.

The growth of community and neighbourhood work was interpreted by the more traditional caseworkers as a threat from a rival discipline rather than an extension of their own role, and the overt political aspirations of many community workers intensified their colleagues' fears. The Home Office described CDP as 'an experiment in methods of promoting social growth—and at all levels, individual, family and community',[15] but John Benington, the respected and widely published leader of the Coventry Project, shortly after attacked the suggestion that community work could be seen as part of a therapy continuum with casework and groupwork.[16] More recently, a growth of interest in systems theory developed an awareness of a unitary approach to social problems, but the tension remains. In inner city departments the majority of social work practitioners continue to perceive their contribution in practice as remedial, crisis-triggered, individual, and focused on the acutely deprived, as distinct from the declared tendency of inner city programmes towards radical, planned and community-wide initiatives.

On the fondness of poverty programmes for small-area projects, social services departments have had mixed feelings.

The Seebohm Report laid the basis for the decentralisation of functions into area teams and in many urban authorities figures much lower than the tentatively suggested 50,000 population have been accepted. Nevertheless, the teams of social workers allocated to a territory rarely have less than ten members and often many more, and the redevelopment of specialisms further militates against the allocation of individual workers to areas as small as a single estate or a few streets. In short, social services are still without any equivalent of the general medical practitioner; for the health service model of primary care to be adopted for social work there would be needed longer training, substantial movement towards the notion of the social worker as an individual professional and considerably more geographical decentralisation and managerial delegation.

The most significant development of the 'patch system' has taken place in Wakefield, a metropolitan if not exactly an inner urban area. In the area team in Normanton, three sub-areas have been established, each with a population of below 7000, staffed by a senior social worker with three patch workers and a domiciliary care organiser, and managing its own home helps, wardens and volunteers.[17] The system is currently being evaluated by a research project from Lancaster University, but it is already claimed that closer identification with a small neighbourhood, the move away from a merely reactive model of helping, the emphasis on the process of 'community enabling' as a first line of action with the counselling service only as a back-up, and the break with the tradition in which 'the referral of an individual problem is the mainspring of team activity' has brought improved working relations with related agencies, a better acceptance of the team by those needing help within the community, and a lowering of the need for crisis intervention. The hope that such a localised system is also appropriate to residential services, which the Wakefield advocates admit implies the development of small homes for all types of clients at an obvious cost to the specifity of the care provided, has yet to be tested.

Few urban authorities have decentralised their fieldwork services to such an extent, but in the London borough of

Islington area teams since Seebohm have served populations as small as 20,000. Aryeh Leissner, building on earlier work on the activities of neighbourhood-based family advice centres,[18] reported in 1974 on the work of one such team which combined in its work service delivery, community organisation and community action. The same stress on availability to the community as a whole was apparent as in the Wakefield work. In both locations the workers realised that they were setting themselves against a tradition of social work addressed to selective clients and, in seeking out the latent strengths of the neighbourhood, were reversing the general tendency of social workers to fix their priorities by the need to get maximum help to those in the most desperate situations.

For the potential client to express his need, he must be able to communicate to the resource controllers, a dialogue constrained on both sides by perceptions of existing provision. For the needy not articulating a demand for services to which he is entitled, through fear, ignorance or simply inertia, can have as damaging an effect on future plans as not being able to recognise his need at all. For this reason, the accessibility of the social service department to its constituency was seen as a prerequisite of effective working in both Wakefield and Islington, and in this there was reflected a consistent thread in thinking on inner city work. In launching CDP, the Home Office commented that people suffering deprivation 'do not know how to gain access to, or to use constructively, the services which exist',[19] and in successive documents since then it has been suggested that workers must achieve a higher level of visibility,[20] that the task of directing those in need to appropriate resources must be given higher priority[21] and that the reception facilities of doctors, social services departments and other helping agencies must express a welcome which frees those who approach them of the stigma historically associated with seeking assistance.[22] The probability that increased activity and take-up will lead to higher costs is less often frankly faced.

Over a decade of discussion there have been marked moves in inner city thinking away from plans geared to specific client groups to an analysis of larger structural faults. The

1977 White Paper *Policy for the Inner Cities*, for example, declares that the heart of the problem is economic decline and the partnerships have attempted to reflect this broadening of the issues by including industrial, commercial and environmental agencies in planning. The increasing complexity of the debate carries disadvantages, however. Local groups and voluntary organisations which generally identify with the needs of clearly defined clusters of people find it difficult to keep up in a world of macro-economic conceptualisation. Unemployment and the decay of the physical infrastructure cannot, realistically, be tackled at the neighbourhood level with which ordinary people and their representatives have been encouraged to identify. Workers in the social services feel the debate to be somehow drifting away into areas to which they and their services are scarcely relevant, a point well expressed—though put a little more positively—by the Director of Social Services for Hackney:

> I wholeheartedly believe that the focus of the Inner City programme should be on improving other aspects of the life of the borough, and that if these were improved, social services would, to some extent, be less necessary.[23]

The recurrent danger as seen by inner city theorists is that people in slums—councillors, social workers, clients, voluntary bodies, neighbourhood groups—will see the programme ultimately as merely the chance to get some extra resources with which to buy marginally more of roughly the same sorts of services they have at the moment. Such concrete incrementalism is strongly represented in the social services, where, as I have tried to demonstrate, the tradition is one of service provision rather than reconstruction, of independent professionalism rather than corporate planning, of action rather than research, of specialist rather than generalised problem-solving, of helping people as individuals or in very small groups rather than *en masse*, of achieving small changes rather than dreaming of new worlds. This is not necessarily the picture social workers would wish to paint of themselves, but it does explain why the White Paper *Policy for the Inner Cities* contains under the heading 'Social Services' just two brief paragraphs!

6

The Planner as Catalyst

Robin Thompson and Andrew Thornley

Should town planners be agents of social action in the inner city or anywhere else? There is a powerful tradition which holds that the profession is concerned only with the regulation of controls and rules for the location, appearance and use of land and buildings. This regulatory role is impartial and apolitical: intervention in the distribution of social services and economic resources between areas or groups is not the business of the town planner. As we shall see, the substance of the legal powers available to planners reinforces this constrained, apolitical perspective.

This traditional approach, however, is under increasing attack. When parts of our cities and sections of our communities are seen to be so manifestly disadvantaged and when positive discrimination becomes a governmental dictate, it is difficult to see why planners should stay on the sidelines. The more so when it can be shown that planning decisions have often exacerbated the disadvantages of the inner city.

Many, though by no means all, planners practising in inner area authorities would favour not only the use of distributional criteria in exercising planning controls, but also direct intervention in the urban system where this can benefit, or prevent disbenefit to, those areas and people most in need and most vulnerable. Like Falstaff, these planners' problem is, 'how greatly desire exceeds performance': the powers to intervene effectively are few and limited.

Certainly it is true that many of the extensive planning

controls over land use introduced by the 1947 Town and Country Planning Act remain: notably the need for permission to undertake development in the forms of new building and of changing the use of existing land and buildings. But for those planners concerned about social change these controls have three main flaws.

Firstly, the capacity of the state to acquire ownership of and appropriate profits from land formed an integral part of the 1947 Act, but has been enfeebled. The Community Land Act, designed to restore some of this capacity, has been remarkably ineffective in the inner areas.

This contributes to the second weakness, the essentially negative or regulatory character of planning powers. Where a local authority does not own land, it can specify what should not be developed on that site; however, it cannot assume that a use it favours will actually be introduced. For example, a development plan may identify an area as suitable for industrial use: citing its plan, the authority could then refuse to allow office or other development, but it could not guarantee that factories would actually be built there.

The third flaw is that the criteria which can be called upon in formulating development plans and development control decisions are generally restricted to physical use of land and to movements between land uses. For example, a residential redevelopment scheme which replaced existing housing could be refused on grounds of its bulk, volume or design, but not because existing low-income tenants are displaced in favour of higher-income tenants in the proposed development.

Although a new planning machinery of strategic structure plans and more detailed local plans was introduced in 1968, it has not proved an adequate remedy for any of these three problems: indeed planners have often damaged their credibility by producing plans which assume a greater capacity to implement their proposals than the planners possess. The past tendency to ignore or undervalue the planners' contribution has given way to concern that their role may need to be strengthened.

Behind the inner city philosophy is the assumption that intervention by the local state is essential if the failure of private enterprise and of other public agencies to invest in the inner city is to be compensated for. Who is to lead these initiatives? The question is unresolved because the synoptic and interventionist role is largely new to local government.

One candidate is the town planner, who, despite the bruises and the shackles, has a relatively broad view, has command of information sources, and is used to dealing with the private sector (especially through development control). Moreover, the modern planner characteristically aspires to discriminate in favour of the disadvantaged. The central point of a local authority's inner city efforts may not always be the planning department (although it very often is), but the demands of the inner city place more onerous responsibilities upon the planners.

However, many practising planners will acknowledge that the inner city problem is rooted in the changing structure of the national and international economy, and that a local authority's contribution will therefore be a marginal one.

Approaches to the inner city problem

There are two broad schools of thought about structural answers. One view holds that the economic decline of these areas is a result of their economic inefficiency and hence their lack of attractiveness to investment. Rather than wasting resources in the fruitless task of counteracting such 'natural' economic forces, the government should foster and encourage industries in their most efficient location. Indeed, the government's industrial strategy is itself designed to restructure and rationalise. This will result, it is argued, in the fastest economic growth for the nation as a whole—which will eventually filter down to everyone, including those living in the inner city. Such an approach may not directly benefit the economies of congested inner areas but the resultant population dispersal would lead to lower land values and lower densities.

This view is the catalyst for the resurrection of planning shibboleths based upon the ideas of such writers as William Morris or Ebenezer Howard: a London of small villages with craftsmen at work within woods and babbling brooks. This approach—encouraging economic forces to find their own efficient pattern and intervening principally through environmental improvements—is that advocated by the Town and Country Planning Association and, to some extent, the Lambeth Inner Area consultants; the former argues:

> The businesses who remain in the inner city areas (though not the central business districts) are increasingly the ones falling by the wayside in our society. We must beware of compounding their plight by attempting to restore the urban pattern of the past for this could only be done by subjecting the poor to still greater pressures upon their living space. The task should be to help the poor more benignly to adjust to the changes that are taking place and hence to the cities of the future . . . We still believe that the problems we now face in the inner city areas are not the result of a failure of dispersal policy *per se* but the result of a failure to make use of the opportunity which dispersal provided.[1]

The alternative approach is that of direct intervention in the economy in favour of inner areas. Intervention could take many forms: one form, of course, is that adopted by the government in its White Paper *Policy for the Inner City*. This states: 'it should be possible now to change the thrust of the policies which have assisted large scale decentralisation'.[2] Thus rather than capitulating to economic forces it would seem that government is bent upon a major programme of intervention and action to create prosperous economies within inner city areas themselves. The government is creating new co-ordinating machinery to make the allocation of resources to the inner city more efficient and effective.

However, within this interventionist strategy, there may be different objectives. The aim could be to overcome the disadvantages such areas have in attracting new investment and simultaneously to generate employment by launching programmes to improvements in infrastructure, transport, industrial land and buildings. Alternatively, the aim could be to make life more bearable for those already living in the area through housing rehabilitation, social welfare or retraining

programmes. The first aim, which could be called the
'regeneration' objective, seeks to improve the relative performance and role of such areas within the city and requires
the influx of economic resources and population, while the
second objective concentrates on action which takes the hard
edge off the problems of living in such areas. The conflict
between these objectives will create strains and tensions
between central government departments, between tiers of
government and between the public bodies and the community.

Given the fact that over 60 per cent of local government
cash is centrally financed, practising planners are conscious
that they must work within the government's inner city
strategy regardless of any reservations. Some may well feel
that the inner city is an inseparable element in the wider
urban economy; they may be aware that more poor people
live outside inner urban areas than live in them; they may, if
they work in towns like Burnley or Hull, wonder how their
problems are less onerous than those of the metropolitan
partnership areas. Be that as it may, Whitehall has the cash
and calls the tune. The tune it is playing is one in which the
structural conflicts are resolved (or rather evaded) by categor-
ising the problem as, substantially, to be found and tackled
in a few small geographical areas.

Small area programmes

The government in this country has a long and unsuccessful
history of tackling the problems of our cities through small
area studies and programmes. We have had, for example, the
urban aid programme, educational priority areas, CDPs, the
'six town studies', the inner area studies, the quality of life
studies', the CCPs and the area management trials.

During the course of these earlier experiences a number of
problems and uncertainties arose. Elected representatives
were not clear about how these special areas fitted into their
traditional role and questioned the interference in their
affairs. The communities themselves were raising demands
that the local authority could not necessarily meet and

requesting greater power and control. Then, most crucially, the strength and importance of interests beyond the small area, beyond the local authority itself, were realised. For example, vital decisions having enormous impact on a specified area could be taken by distant company boardrooms. The Canning Town CDP has shown how the boardroom reaction of the largest sugar company in the world to EEC controls and a shift from cane refining to beet production could result in devastating effects upon the Canning Town community.[3] The message from the programmes (most cogently expressed in the CDP reports) is that the causes of the problems cannot be ascribed to particular individuals nor yet to particular areas or local authorities but to the broader functioning of the economic system. Thus any action that is confined to these areas and does not relate to these broader forces will, at best, be a temporary palliative, and serve to 'contain' problems for a short while only.

Do the same limitations apply to the inner city programmes? It would appear so. The way in which the inner city programme was announced and the major objectives stressed indicate considerable continuity with previous small area programmes. Government ministers introducing the new policy direction at the beginning of 1977 stressed continually that this was not a programme of massive new resources but one of management: to make more efficient use of existing resources. 'Comprehensive', 'co-ordinated', 'cohesive', 'integrated', 'committed' were the key words. The aim was to get everyone (all central and local government departments and other agencies such as the police, health authorities and passenger transport authorities) to work together with voluntary bodies in a common programme.

A second major theme was stressed at the interception of the programme, although it is referred to far less now. This can be called 'tension management': it seeks to prevent the outbreak of unrest in areas that are suffering the worst effects of the economic crisis, high concentrations of unemployment and depressing environmental conditions. Race riots, crime and vandalism are the indicators of the potential threat. As Reg Freeson, then Minister of Housing, warned at a conference in early 1977,[4] such problems could spread to neighbouring areas and affect people living 'productive ordinary lives'. The Tory Reform Group cogently expresses the view in the following way:

> . . . the threat of social unrest and disturbance becomes more real as the poverty gap widens. People are already prepared to take the law into their own hands, for example, by squatting. A more alarming danger is that simmering racial tension could erupt unless more is done for the inner cities because that is where black people in this country tend to concentrate.[5]

Thus two pragmatic objectives were at the centre of the government's inner city programme from the outset—the more efficient juggling of existing resources through better management, and the control of potential unrest. To these restricted aims the government has directed ever more modest resources. How have planners responded to the restricted, and purely pragmatic, aims of the government's inner city programmes? What scope have they been able to find within the programmes to address the *causes* of the problem, not merely its symptoms?

Inner area programmes

It is worth at this point examining the efforts being made within the mainstream of the government strategy: examples are drawn from the Lambeth construction money allocation and the Hackney/Islington partnership programme.

Lambeth received an allocation of £5 million for construction works to take place between 1977 and 1979. Over £3 million of this was allocated to housing rehabilitation and modernisation of Lambeth and GLC estates. Of the remainder £1 million was to be spent on homes for handicapped children and the rest on small environmental and social projects. The main feature of this programme is the strong emphasis on housing improvement and the insignificant economic element: Lambeth has used this money to top up its main programmes rather than to innovate. Rehabilitation programmes have suffered recently from public expenditure cuts and the construction money was seen as an opportunity to remedy this loss.

Not all construction money has been spent in this way, of course: other authorities such as Liverpool and Birmingham have spent more on employment-oriented projects and the London Docklands have emphasised transport and infrastructure. Nevertheless, all have been constrained by the short time allowed to prepare the expenditure programme and the inelasticity of local government financing and implementation.

The production in early 1978 of the Hackney/Islington *Themes and Priorities* paper was the first step in the preparation of their inner area programme. Guy Barnett, a junior minister at the Department of the Environment, writing in the foreword states: 'The retention and creation of employment activities and prosperity for the inhabitants of the Borough should be identified as the clear priority for the partnership.' The paper then sets out the possible action programmes and asks for public comment. The list of possibilities is restricted to conventional projects with an emphasis on physical improvements and shifting priorities to certain client groups within the existing local authority programme structure. On the employment side the suggestions are confined to counselling and liaison activities between local authority, employers and schools and to provision of adequate industrial premises with a plea for 'sympathetic operation of industrial development'.

The forword's advocacy of economic regeneration is not reflected in a list of possible action, which lacks innovative thought and reflects the pressure from departments and agencies which wish to use the partnership to implement all those pet schemes that have been gathering dust on the office shelves since the expenditure cuts began. This 'first step' is as limited as the Lambeth construction package. It certainly does not stretch the role and responsibility within the economic field of the planner or local authority. In the remainder of this chapter we will explore some of the alternative courses of action through which more ambitious projects may be achieved.

New directions

These alternative courses of action have to be considered
within the context of the economic forces which cause inner
city decline and of the government's attempts to bolster the
national economy. Central government, in striving for national
prosperity, will support profitable and efficient enterprises
(cf. the industrial strategy) and this will often exacerbate the
problems of unemployment in inner city areas. Central
government has to ensure that problems in these areas do not
reach dangerous proportions and this puts in perspective its
pragmatic approach to the inner city.

We have seen that the planners' traditional prescriptive role
is constrained by its largely spatial and negative nature.
Nevertheless, statutory plans and formal implementation of
planning laws can make a contribution. The local plans now
being produced in cities do bring together and update policies
for location of housing, economic activities, shops and other
land uses; their regulative policies can be helpful—for
example, in co-ordinating public transport with those uses
which generate large flows of people and goods; plans must
go through processes of public consultation; and they can
eliminate blight and uncertainty.

A further resource available to planners is that of information. The way in which information is selected and analysed
can have a strong influence on policy-making. For example,
some authorities have established registers of available
industrial land and buildings in their area, or have set up
business advice centres to advise on grants, tax concessions
or job opportunities. Planners can also adopt an advocative
role that acknowledges the limits of their powers but
persuades the local authority to use its influence and command of information to suggest policies for other bodies to
pursue.

The work on industrial improvement in Rochdale provides
an interesting example of planners using an opportunistic
combination of traditional powers and the additional tools of
promotion, information and advocacy. The Crawford Street
Area covers 50 hectares near the centre of Rochdale and
exhibits a characteristic mixture of poor housing, obsolescent

industrial building and infrastructure, and poor circulation and services. In response planners have developed a sound though unexceptional land-use plan. The decision to declare it an Industrial Improvement Area provided an indication of local authority concern and served to encourage potential investors.

In addition to its own slum clearance and physical renovation programme, the authority involved local industrialists through a survey and consultation machinery which included the Area Steering Group. Potential investors were also informed about a wide variety of possible support ranging from derelict land grants to EEC infrastructure grants. Whilst the input of public resources was fairly modest and often spent on cosmetic environmental improvements rather than more expensive infrastructure, the returns to Rochdale's activist approach were relatively impressive. The Rochdale planners argue: 'the promotional/selling aspect of the IIA project cannot be stressed too highly'.[6] The Rochdale scheme won the Royal Town Planning Institute's Silver Jubilee Cup, beating off competition from the more orthodox battery of schemes to prettify historic town centres: a singular sign of the times.

This experiment influenced the government in the preparation of its Inner Urban Areas Act, which confers additional powers on inner city areas with special social needs. These special powers allow the local authority to make loans for land-acquisition and site-preparation, or for improvement of amenities or buildings in designated industrial improvement areas, and provide grants towards the rent of industrial buildings. Meanwhile the major conurbation authorities (for example, West Midlands, Tyne and Wear, Merseyside and the Greater London Council) have been seeking, in Special Powers Bills placed before Parliament, economic powers that go further than this. These powers would include permission for local authorities to take equity shares in local firms and to establish their own enterprises geared to local needs and local skills: for example, to make school uniforms or to provide a network of butchers shops in more isolated housing estates. Although these powers have not always been granted, they presage a local authority desire for a stronger role in the local economy. The powers sought are more extensive than those in the Inner Urban Areas Act. Whereas those in the Act are concerned with the financial help a local authority could provide through loans and grants, the metropolitan authorities are striving for ways they can actually *control* the local economy either through direct involvement with their own enterprises or through partnership with particular local firms. This difference is a recent reflection at the local level of a change of attitude in national economic planning from the provision of grants and loans—for example, regional incentives—to government involvement in particular industries—for example, through the NEB and planning agreements.

Funding for these newer forms of activity by a local authority encounters the parsimony of the Treasury and the inelasticity of local government accounting. The few areas of relatively independent spending available to Town Halls, such as the locally determined sector, have been particularly savagely cut in recent times. However, resourceful authorities have 'found' money either by redirection of services or by investigating dusty corners. Section 137 of the Local Government Act allows the use of the product of a two-penny rate for any useful purpose and this has been used for industrial promotion. South Yorkshire intends to use 5 per cent of its superannuation fund to support local businesses. Firms acquiring industrial premises can be given industrial mortgages, and authorities in the Intermediate Areas have applied to the EEC's Regional Development Fund and to the European Investment Bank.

It is not surprising that these metropolitan authorities should be seeking the means by which they can have a greater say in the economic life of their areas. Any reduction in the reliance of a local area on a multinational, a monopoly, or a large national enterprise will reduce the dangers of sudden economic catastrophe for local people and provide a firmer base for locally determined social programmes.

Some programmes that local authorities are considering (not necessarily through Special Powers Acts) seem to offer a substantial contribution to the inner city problem that is related to the real *cause* of the problem itself.

In a recent paper R. Minns and J. Thornley described three

initiatives that a local authority could take: taking out shares in local firms; supporting workers' co-operatives; or undertaking municipal enterprise itself. Certain authorities have already bought share capital in local firms: Greater Manchester Council set up its own company to develop land and buildings which provides loans, guarantees and equity capital for smaller firms. According to Minns and Thornley:

> The main advantage of share holding is its pump-priming nature. With a relatively small input of risk capital, the local authority can help make a small firm viable and improve its capital structure so that it can attract future investment from private sources.[7]

This form of local authority intervention can influence the location of economic activities and the production and workforce policies of companies. Minns and Thornley suggest that a Municipal Enterprise Board could be set up to co-ordinate the commercial operations of a local authority.

Some authorities have offered financial support for workers' co-operatives or established a special revolving loan fund set aside for the promotion of local co-operatives. The control and future of the enterprises should remain in the hands of the local authority and local people. A network of co-operatives could provide a more stable base for the local economy along the lines successfully pursued in parts of Italy.

A third area of innovation is that of direct local authority activity. This can be through the establishment of its own direct labour force, or the expansion of local authority employment to reduce local unemployment. The authority can adapt its own recruitment policies to reflect the needs of the local labour force, as the London Borough of Camden has done in reviewing its hiring policies to ensure equal access to ethnic minorities. The local authority is an important consumer of goods and services—for example, office stationery, school equipment, building materials and services such as office-cleaning. Many of these needs are met at present on the open market. There may be an opportunity here for careful placement of contracts or local tendering to favour local firms, even if it is impossible to municipalise their activities.

It is through a co-ordinated approach that most benefit will be achieved: municipal enterprise in certain limited areas, linked to a policy of loans, contracts and tenders to favour the local-authority-sponsored co-operatives and those firms in which the authority has an equity stake. Such an integrated approach—a local economic strategy in which the local authority has a central role—could be a major step towards greater economic stability in inner city areas.

The application of new powers and initiatives

This advance of planning into areas beyond its direct influence and control is an essential and developing contribution to inner area policy and, indeed, to general intervention in favour of the disadvantaged. However, local authorities have limited experience in these pioneering efforts and some confusion is already detectable. The priority afforded to the stimulation of local economies is an appropriate response to the underlying inner area malaise. But what sort of jobs should be encouraged? The rush to grab manufacturing work of any kind may overlook the needs, potential and limitations of the local economy and workforce. Neighbouring authorities are often competing against each other rather than agreeing which specific contributions each can offer to the city's general economic revival. Few have decided which economic activities they can most usefully promote: in some areas service industries may offer the most realistic growth prospects and may provide jobs at least as well paid and as well suited to local workers as those in manufacturing.

The conflicts which can arise between economic involvement and other objectives of inner city policy have also been too little considered. A housing policy which seeks to encourage a satisfactory workforce must also contend with the priority required for assisting those groups in greatest need—groups which will include large numbers of children and the elderly, who are economically inactive. Business demands for adequate access, servicing areas and parking may conflict with the desire to limit private traffic in order to support the public transport upon which the poorer and less mobile groups are especially dependent.

All of these limitations require a second dimension to the planner's activity. Intervention and promotion at the local level is necessary, but it must be related to a strategic overview of the economic and other planning priorities at national, regional and city level. This is one of the synoptic skills which planners should particularly be able to offer and a skill which correlates closely with their efforts in the fields of information and advocacy. The task of developing a common strategic overview involving several tiers of government, at national and local levels, and the private sector is a formidable one. No one is better equipped than the planner to perform this task, and without it the hard work and enterprise already devoted to revitalisation at the local level will lose much of its direction and much of its impact.

Part 3
Community
Perspectives

7

Housing for People

Ron Bailey

The 'housing issue', the 'housing question', the 'housing problem': these terms and many more are bandied around freely by the providers of housing—central government, local authorities and housing associations—and campaigners for improvements and reform alike. They indicate, perhaps, only one thing: that despite all the concern and all the promises of recent years—and haven't there been plenty of both of those?—there still is a housing issue/question/problem. Certainly the mere fact that everybody uses the same terms should not be taken as any indication that there is a unity of view about the solutions needed or, less ambitiously, about the paths towards those solutions. Indeed, it is easy to get the impression—and many of the homeless people that I have been in contact with certainly have it—that the most important thing to many people is that they prove that their solutions are right.

Some people, for instance, believe that the Rent Acts with their rent control and security of tenure clauses need to be changed. People who view this as any kind of solution are usually called, by those who don't, 'dyed-in-the-wool Tories', 'reactionaries' and other such terms. Others believe that the answer lies in more municipalisation and more public spending. These people are usually called, by the 'dyed-in-the-wool Tories', 'doctrinaire socialists', 'Marxist dogmatists' and the like.

All these groups, however, have two errors in common.

Firstly, they doubt the genuine concern of the other groups. The 'dyed-in-the-wool Tories' believe that the 'doctrinaire socialists' and the 'Marxist dogmatists' don't *really* care for the homeless and the badly housed, but that they are only using them to propagate their views. From my experience this is manifestly untrue. The people who work in the Law Centres, the community work organisations, the housing campaigns (and they are usually on the political left) certainly do care about the problem, and those who doubt this are blind.

Similarly, however, the 'doctrinaire socialists' and the 'Marxist dogmatists' are wrong on their often-held belief that the 'dyed-in-the-wool Tories' don't care. They usually do— and just as much. I have spoken to them and I believe that they, or at least most of them, want the 1974 Rent Act amended, *not* because they want to see the badly housed in dire straits so that the landlords can get rich, but because they genuinely believe that in the long run this will actually be in the interest of the badly housed. It is almost a heresy in some circles to say this, but I believe that many of the 'dyed-in-the-wool Tories' actually care just as much as many of the 'doctrinaire socialists' or 'Marxist dogmatists'.

The second error that both groups have in common is that by and large—and I admit there are exceptions to this—they have a similar view of the problem: there are not enough houses to go round in the right place at the right cost in the right condition. That, to most people in the groups mentioned above, is the extent of the problem, the question then being 'how do we solve it?' so that the differing answers follow on from the same definition of the issues at stake. At a first glance it would seem obvious that this definition of the problem is what it is all about—and yet I am aware that I have called it an error! I hope to explain that more fully later.

For the moment I want to return to the 'caring' point. I have argued that the socialists, the Marxists *and* the Tories all care equally, and that in effect no group has a monopoly of concern. I have argued that their solutions stem from genuine concern. However, that is not to say that the solutions they come up with are not fettered by their prejudices.

By that I mean that the limits of the solution that are acceptable to each group are governed by their preconceived party
political stances. The three groups, therefore—the Tories, the
socialists and the Marxists—while all having a genuine concern,
are hidebound, as regards what they can accept as a solution,
by their politics. That is not to question their concern.
Rather it is to question the usefulness of *all* their politics.
Rather it is to say that their politics to a greater or lesser
extent—and the amount will vary depending upon the person,
the time, the issue—actually nullify their genuine human
feelings of concern.

One small indication of the way in which preconceived
traditional political ideas govern one's view of the situation,
and thus the solutions, can actually be seen in this book. The
editors have called Part I 'The Political Framework'; and they
have included three contributions—Conservative, Labour and
Marxist. It is no accident that these are the traditional
political divisions; but are they really the only three elements
of the 'framework'? I don't think so: in fact I think that the
(albeit implied) view that they are is *actually part of the
housing problem.*

And so we return to the problem itself. I have already
stated that I believe the traditional concept of this to be
erroneous—although incomplete would be a better word,
because obviously the lack of the right type of houses in the
right places is a problem. But equally the constraining nature
of the traditional political concepts is a problem because, as
stated, it affects one's suggestions for solutions. There is,
however, another whole classification of problems which
has not yet been touched upon, but which is vitally important
to any discussion of action designed to solve, either in part
or in whole, housing problems. I am refering here to issues
which can be grouped under the heading 'quality of life'.
This term covers a multitude of things so I will explain what
I mean by it by example rather than by definition.

Recently I have been visiting people who have been
rehoused following local authority action under Part III of
the 1957 Housing Act—that is, slum clearance. They have
described to me their previous living conditions—tiny rooms,
inadequate natural lighting, damp, WC at the bottom of the

garden, no hot water and no bath, no electric lighting and so on. In short they have described all the traditional features of bad housing that slum clearance programmes were designed to alleviate. They have also shown me round their present accommodation with its bright rooms, hot and cold water, and the rest. And then I have talked to them of their feelings.

> I've never cried so much as in the past four years since I was rehoused.

> I've forgotten what it's like to talk to people.

> We never had 'the Welfare' in those days and we didn't need them. If I was ill I'd give the key to my neighbour who'd do the shopping, come in and clean up and make dinner for me.

> You didn't need someone calling every week to see if you were OK. If you were stuck indoors someone was sure to knock and if you really did need [outside] help they'd get it.

> Old Mr So-and-So used to sit on his front step—it was as far as he could walk. He'd talk to everyone as they went by. It was his life.

All this and more: statements—feelings—by people who supposedly no longer have a housing problem, as they are rehoused in modern conditions. Indeed, I have also heard it said that 'I wish I were back where I came from'. Whether or not the people believe this themselves, or whether or not they would like it if they were whisked back, is not the point. Every one of those statements is an indication that the traditional view of the housing problem is inadequate; every one of those statements describes a different kind of housing problem; and every one of those people who made those statements has a housing problem—although they are adequately housed. And let me add that they were not made by people living in tower blocks, which it is now generally accepted are unsuitable at least for families.

A major part, therefore, of today's housing problem is that even where people are adequately housed, they are desperately unhappy, they feel no sense of belonging. I read once a description of work by a Ford worker. He wrote:

> on an assembly line a man can work day after day for years on end only a few yards from a workmate, yet neither will know anything of each other. They will often not even speak to each other—the few yards might as well be miles separating them.[1]

The same is true of many modern housing developments. It was Marx who wrote 'when the worker is at work he is not at home', but for many perfectly adequately housed people today it is true that 'when the person is at home he/she is not at home'.

Alienation, then, is as much a problem of housing today as are conditions; and those whose sole perspectives are concerned with conditions do nothing to get to grips with this problem.

There are, therefore, three prongs of the housing problem—three issues, or rather three parts of the same issue, which must be tackled: bad housing in the traditional sense; alienation; and politics in the traditional sense. What can be done about it?

The housing issue is only one issue in society; housing is merely part of society as a whole. It would be simple to say, therefore, that society itself must be changed before these issues can really be dealt with. That, however, is too glib and too easy. We need to talk about what we can do now to start the process of dealing with the housing problem. So we need to discuss what actions we can take in the immediate future.

The squatting and self-help housing movement is the most obvious example of a current housing movement that combines action on all three fronts—the scarcity front, the alienation front and the 'political' front. The movement arose out of the homeless hostel struggle of the 1960s. In this the homeless families took united action not just to secure better conditions but to challenge the right of local authorities to make rules as they saw fit. Thus the campaign challenged, for instance, rules about no husbands being allowed into the hostels, and about restrictions in the lives of the occupants.

The local authorities resisted the campaign, but the campaign was successful. Out of this success the current squatting campaigns started in 1968. By definition these were not merely campaigns for better conditions in people's existing accommodation; they were campaigns against the right of local authorities—initially—to leave houses empty. Once again, despite the opposition of local authorities, these campaigns were successful.

Before discussing this success, however, it is worth pausing to consider the opposition from the councils. Kent County Council jailed husbands for sleeping with their wives during the 1966 campaign at King Hill hostel; Redbridge Council employed a gang cf hired thugs to remove squatters in 1969; Tower Hamlets Council would not talk to squatters for a year in 1970; Southwark Council systematically vandalised hundreds of its own houses in an effort to stop squatters in 1971.

It is worth asking why? Were Kent, Redbridge, Tower Hamlets and Southwark Councils full of evil people who had no concern for the homeless? Well, maybe. But I think that is too simple an answer. I am sure many people who get on to local councils, or who start work in local government, do so because they want to put their energies into helping people. Because they are 'concerned'. So what goes wrong? There are, I believe, four main problems. Firstly, concern is often equated with the need for power—albeit power to do something about the things which concern them. The councillors and officers in Kent, Redbridge, Tower Hamlets and Southwark had obtained that power, and then were anxious not to have their housing policies, formulated because of their concern over the problem, obstructed. Thus they tried to clamp down on the protestors, who resisted, with the result that in the end the concerned councils were doing quite abominable things.

Secondly, once people move in circles where power is executed, they all too easily slip into needing to be strong, so that they can retain their position to carry on with their good policies. Thus in Lambeth in 1977 the battle over the demolition of squatted houses in St Agnes Place ceased to be about the rival merits of demolition over renovation. Instead it degenerated into a factional fight between rival wings of the Labour Party in which the most important factor became the need for the council leadership to avoid losing face publicly.

Thirdly, those in power think they have the right to rule, and in traditional political terms they are right. Further, the whole democratic system enhances this belief as it gives it moral authority. Thus, Southwark Council could reject the squatting proposals for the use of empty houses on the grounds that if they accepted them they 'would be put in the position of having to share the administration of [their] housing policy and the management of [their] properties with people who "have a special interest in the matter" '.[2] And that would be anathema. To a greater or lesser extent that kind of thinking was behind—is behind—all the seemingly unbelievably harsh actions of those who got to power because they were concerned.

Finally, those in power convince themselves that they have to do certain things because they have no alternative. Thus if they spend more on housing, they will have less to spend on education; thus they are forced to agree to the current cuts because there just isn't the money in the kitty. They *are* concerned, but they have to face reality and do their best in an imperfect world. In their terms everything can be justified.

The success of the hostel and squatting campaigns was that they successfully challenged all these assumptions. The people involved decided that they themselves were, for once, going to make the decisions affecting their lives. They didn't give a damn about the plans of those in power; they didn't give a damn when their pleas turned to bullying; they didn't give a damn about the discomfiture of the politicians and their explanation that they wanted to help but couldn't or, the politicians' justification that they had to oppose the campaign in the general interest of the rest of the public. The hostel families and the squatters decided that they were going to decide what to do about hostel conditions and empty houses rather than the councils.

The result has been that the practice of taking children into care because of homelessness has declined because of the hostel campaign; the support which central government now gives to schemes for using short-life empty property and the practice of many local authorities of using some at least of their empty properties for the homeless, rather than the old workhouse-type institution, are direct results of the hostel and squatting campaigns; the recent Greater London Council amnesty for all squatters, which also for the first time gives single people a major claim on public accommodation, was a direct result of the widespread squatting in empty GLC property. Years before, the GLC had tacitly accepted that they couldn't possible cope with it and the practice of the officers was to leave squatters in occupation at least until they needed the houses. The new amnesty formalised this and took it further when squatters were rehoused in empty permanent accommodation.

In fact, the improvements in national policy regarding homelessness and empty houses have come about in the last decade because of campaigns which not only demanded better conditions, but challenged the authorities' assumed right to decide, and were carried on *outside and despite* the traditional political channels.

There have, in addition to these struggles, been, year in, year out, struggles by ordinary people to protect their communities. Many of the people uprooted from their homes because of 'slum clearance' have ended up unhappy and lonely—and word has got around. So now local authority 'slum clearance' compulsory purchase orders are often bitterly opposed by people not wanting to be cleared.

To many local authorities slum clearance has become a numbers game, or a bureaucratic tidy-up: the so-called slums are not cleared because people want to move out, but either because the numbers of 'slums' demolished will put the council higher up the league table, or because the homes actually do offend some rule that the local environmental health officer wishes to enforce. And, of course, he or she is so right—after all, these houses *do* break the rules (or else they wouldn't be slums) and it is the duty of the council to ensure that people do not live in slums! Indeed it is—but is it the duty of the council to move people out of homes in which they want to live? It is once again a matter of who has the right to rule—the state in all its wisdom and with its concern for people living in inferior housing, or the people themselves? There is no doubt where the power lies. Providing the state can show that homes are 'slums', then they can get the inhabitants out—whatever the inhabitants want. Indeed, it has been ruled in the High Court that the destruction of a sense of community by a local authority clearance programme is not a reason for halting the council's plans. In other words, if they say the people must go, they know best.

This has been the practice up and down the country whichever political party is in power, and however strong the desire of the local authority officers to help people. But fortunately there have been successful fights against the machine—and these have taken place outside the traditional political parties. In Leicester and in Lambeth, for instance, people not wanting to be cleared have successfully opposed slum clearance operations. And there is no doubt that the present national policy of rehabilitation rather than demolition was brought about, in part at least, by the widespread (but diverse) protest movements against demolition.

Campaigns against 'town centre redevelopment' have also been bitterly fought in many parts of the country. These have been the battleground of people-versus-planners struggles—and a feature of most of them has been the quality of life; the corner shop versus the supermarket, the ribbon of shops along the main street versus the enclosed multi-storey shopping precinct.

In many people's eyes this has been a life (with all its faults) versus death (with all its planned perfection) struggle. Most of these struggles have been unsuccessful—because the Town Hall machines hold all the aces—the power, the staff, the law, the participation games, even the public inquiry system. All those work to the benefit of 'them'. Yes—even the independent public inquiries. The machines usually win—how can they lose with their unlimited staff and their full-time experts? Any planner can easily demonstrate the benefits of a shopping precinct over a ribbon development—warmth, protection from rain, easy accessibility, geographical proximity and so on. Shopping centres need cars, of course, and once again innumerable multi-storey car parks can easily be shown to be necessary. And new town centres, it is hoped,

attract more trade, which will increase rateable value and so
help the people of the borough; but more trade means more
traffic, which will congest the already overcrowded existing
roads, so a by-pass is needed with special service roads to the
shops. It is a planner's dream; it is perfection and it is an
unanswerable case—provided you eliminate or ignore the
people, both those living in the 500 or more houses that
have to be smashed down to make way for perfection and
those who have watched the destruction of their old town
High Street. And what is the result of the (almost) inevitable
victory for such plans at any public inquiry? The creation of
a perfect concrete desert where no one goes at night (unless
they're brave!) where no one knows anyone else, let alone
talks to them, and where the whole perfect environment is
created on a drawing board.

But are public inquiries the farce that I have implied? Is
it not possible to win against the machine? Maybe it is—just.
Take the London Borough of Redbridge, for instance. The
council dreamt up a town centre plan for Ilford in the 1960s.
It involved the demolition of 1000 houses, and over 2000
local people objected. They studied the plan, they studied
the planners, they put in an enormous amount of time and
effort. They matched the council expert for expert. They
paid for representation at the public inquiry in 1970. And
they won: they beat the council machine. That is what
happened in theory—the practice was rather different. Even
before the inquiry the council had flattened large chunks of
central Ilford; and after the inquiry—they went on doing
exactly the same thing. The council had lost the inquiry—so
they went on demolishing the area. The council machine
has coughed up another plan now and there are two public
inquiries pending. They will win these—there's hardly
anybody left in central Ilford to resist. So much for victory
at a public inquiry.

A similar story can be reported from south wales. A
recent study of town centre plans and public inquiries in
Swansea revealed:

At the Quadrant inquiry the Council said that foundation
work—services—had already started and the contract for

the multi-storey car park already let. On December 16th
1975 the main contract with Debenhams and C.I.N. was
signed five months before the inquiry. People's rights in
planning are meagre enough under the present laws. The
Swansea story shows how they can, all very legally, be
completely and step by step nullified . . . The lesson is that
if you are dependent upon Public Inquiries you will lose.[3]

But who can complain? The objectors have had their
voices heard and no doubt the inspectors did their best to be
fair. The basic point is that fairness and the whole system just
do not go together. The machine beats the system because
the system is switched into the machine. The people are the
losers—whether they 'win' or 'lose'.

The people displaced cannot complain either! They are
rehoused in nice modern accommodation where they know
nobody, talk to nobody and cry; where they have no affinity
with or control over their immediate environment, and where
their every move, almost, is subject to planning legislation. A
new garden shed, a few pigeons in the loft, a makeshift
garage, all features of the life of ordinary people: but in their
new perfect accommodation all these become subject to
planning legislation, which, like slum clearance legislation,
was initially enacted to help people but too often has become
a weapon in the hands of the machine—only to be used in the
interests of the people, of course.

And even where people in their modern homes can get
permission to build a shed or a wall or whatever, it is only
after asking and filling in the right forms in the right way.
People's idiosyncracies, their quirks, their interests, their
whole lives have become institutionalised. I have heard it said
that people these days are becoming too dependent upon
what is provided for them. Is it any wonder when one has to
get permission in triplicate to exercise initiative? Dependence
is easier, and it is likely to meet with greater approval,
because it is 'fileable' and fits into the system more easily.

The meaning of all this is that in conventional political
terms people are disenfranchised—and they know it and react
accordingly. It is called 'apathy'; perhaps it is apathy—or
perhaps it is simply that they are fed up with a system that

they know does not work in their favour.

The prospects for real action in the housing field do not lie in the 'democratic' system, therefore, because this simply puts one group in control, and then another group, and so on. Those who gain control in this way, however well meaning, do not give people any more control over their environment.

The only way to tackle *all three* parts of the housing problem is for people themselves to build up their own organisations and movements *outside* the normal political structure. The minute people do this they will see where their friends and foes are; they will see most of the politicos who bemoan apathy, describing them as 'irresponsible' and urging them not to be 'mislead'. They will see, in fact, that party politics is the enemy of the people. It is true, of course, that some people in the political parties will support movements of ordinary working people—but this is more *despite* their party allegiance than because of it.

It is not the role of activists and committed people, therefore, to urge people to get involved in the democratic system or to join political parties. Indeed, it is more the case that the extent to which people's protest and action are directed into the normal channels is the extent to which the whole system will continue. And if the system continues the housing problem will continue. It is possible—and I put it no stronger than that—that the present system can solve the scarcity element of the housing problem, but it cannot by its very nature overcome the alienation issue and it cannot by its very nature rid us of the hidebound thinking of the political parties; these are integral parts of the (democratic) system.

These problems can only be overcome by actions by ordinary people themselves, outside the system (although on occasions it may be necessary to use parts of the system to manipulate it). The extent to which they take such actions and organise such movements is the extent to which *they* will solve the housing problem. This will, in the end, involve a fundamental change in the control structure of society; but the process can start immediately. Wherever there are rules which oppress people, or plans which destroy them or scarcity which leaves them in appalling conditions, people can fight back. And the extent to which they are successful will be determined by the strength of their organisations and their movements. Small demands can be won in this way; some power can be taken back; some bad conditions can be ended. The present system will bend and it will make concessions; as already indicated pressure can work, even for purely short-term gains; or to bring about changes in national policy, widespread public pressure and protest works. Thus a movement outside the normal channels loses none of the immediate 'goodies'—in fact, it often brings them into existence. In addition it is the only way to solve the alienation problem. And unless we want an affluent well-housed prison-like society *that* is what must be tackled.

8

Claimants in Action*

Jean Whitfield in collaboration with Bill Jordan

It's the red, white and blue making war on the poor,
And blind mother justice on a pile of manure.
(Song by Richard and Mimi Farina)

Scene: Plymouth Social Security Office
Date: 19 May 1978

MAN: But I've signed on.

SUPERVISOR: They said your signing on time is 2.15, Mr Batten. They just said so.

MAN: But I've signed on. I told you. I signed on—I signed on at 11 o'clock this morning. I did.

SUPERVISOR: Well, it's not enough. Your time is 2.15.

MAN (*stammering and near to tears*): But I've signed on. I've signed on already.

CLAIMANTS UNION MEMBER (*Walks into the cubicle uninvited and leans over hands on the counter*): If it's a question of this gentleman needing money over the counter, if he's in urgent need and if he's already signed on, then

---

* All incidents described in this chapter are factual but names have been changed in all cases.

it's in the '76 Act that it's his right to receive it. And he says he *has* signed on.

SUPERVISOR (*changing from being firm to growing angry*): It's not as easy as that. There are other things to . . . we've got our rules and regulations . . . the unemployment have just phoned . . . they phoned me, I didn't phone them, they got into contact with me and they said (*she's thumping one hand up and down in the air*) he's to sign on at 2.15.

MAN: But I've signed on. I signed on at 11 this morning. (*Turns his head from side to side.*)

CU: Have you got anything to show them when you have to sign on?

MAN (*scrabbling at a heap of folded pieces of paper*): Yes. Here. (*He produces a yellow card with a column of days. Against Thursday is the time 11 a.m.*)

CU: There it is—it says here 11 a.m. on Thursdays. Today *is* Thursday. He signed on this morning and now he needs a giro to pay for this week. It's a payment over the counter. He's in urgent need of it and a section in the Act covers it. (*She's thinking, thank God he had that bit of paper. It ought to be fairly straightforward now . . . You'd think he was asking for the moon.*)

SUPERVISOR (*shouting now; no pretence at firm polite authority left. Later someone asked: 'Who was that woman screaming in the interview cubicle?'*): I've told you it's not as easy as that—we've got our rules and regulations . . .

CU But they're not the law . . .

SUPERVISOR (*shaking with fury*): We aren't just here to pay out money you know—and don't you try telling me what's the law— *I* know what's the law and what isn't—if we were, we'd just heap up a pile of money (*she's flinging her arms around again*) in the middle of that room (*she means the waiting room*) and let them fight for it, take it away . . . (*walking away*).

CU (*loudly, pushing the yellow form forward, thinking, oh Christ*): Look, it says here this gentleman signs on at 11 a.m. on Thursday. He's signed on and he's entitled to a payment over the counter. Now. He needs the money now.

SUPERVISOR (*shouting, shouting*): And I've just told you

that that's not enough (*she's disappearing beyond the partition*). They just phoned me . . .

CU: Well, now you've seen this form ring them back and check and then make the payment.

SUPERVISOR (*sarcastically*): It's not *my* job to ring them up all the time—it's his job to walk to the dole office and sign on . . .

MAN: But I've signed on already. I told you. I've signed on. I signed.

SUPERVISOR (*closing her eyes and compressing her lips*): . . . and sign on again or is he just too . . . can't he be bothered to walk just round the corner to sign on? (*The dole office is at the other end of the city centre, but never mind. She steps through the door to the inner office and slides it, slams it shut.*)

(*Pause. Silence.*)

CU My God.

MAN (*red in the face—nearly in tears—his hands waving emptily, quietly, weakly—it's almost funny*): But I've signed on.

CU: Well, best thing—(*thinking, that supervisor's in the frame of mind to get the police, and this man's got enough to worry about*)—go down there; sign on again if you can; get them to ring her and don't come away without getting it in writing that you've signed on once today already and that your correct time is clearly down for her to see. Then come back and claim a payment over the counter.

MAN (*holds his head in his hands*): I don't know what to do. This is the fourth time . . .

CU: Look, read this out when you get back here. (*She writes on a scrap of paper a sentence from Section 4 of the 1976 Act. The sentence reads, 'Nothing . . . shall prevent payment of benefit in an urgent case.'*)

MAN: Thank you. (*He is nodding and crying and repeating 'Thank you' and going down the narrow passage. He is penniless.*) I read this out? Thank you (*He turns round, puts up his hand, tries to smile but his face is twisted.*) OK.
 (*The door swings shut.*)

Note: The Plymouth Claimants Union, like other Claimants

Unions, has as part of its explicit policy members present at local social security offices. It must be remembered that claimants—some 60 per cent of whom are pensioners—have little or no support in these confrontations. Very few claimants have social workers to support them; even fewer have social workers able to take time or prepared to make time to go with them to the offices; and fewer still are the social workers who have ever had welfare rights as part of their training so that they know what are the important questions to ask and statements to make.

Not that the story ends there: Claimants Union members also attend appeal tribunals . . .

Scene: Appeal Tribunal
Date: July 1976

   (*The Chairman, a stout, benign, grey-haired man, is summing up.*)

CHAIRMAN (he speaks kindly, paternally—but there is a hint of steel): Have you anything more to say? We understand and sympathise that your children have no wet-weather clothing and we note that they have no nightwear.

JIM (*claimant*): We've none of us any outdoor clothes. I haven't any and my wife hasn't either. It's not just the children.

CLAIMANTS UNION MEMBER: And Mr Perks's wife is suffering from a long-term thyroid complaint. I should like the tribunal to make a note of that. In addition, neither Mr Perks nor his wife knew or was told that a weekly addition *can* be made if someone's ill.

JIM: And these shoes . . . (*he moves his chair back to show his shoes but the teak table is too wide and heavy for anyone to see; only the CU member and the social security officer can see where the soles have come away from the uppers*) . . . and these shoes let water. They're hopeless.

LADY (*a member of the Tribunal, she's small and quiet and hasn't said anything or changed her expression throughout the tribunal, which has lasted about forty minutes. Now she leans forward, cutting Jim short on the subject of his*

shoes. She has a distinct 'Children's Hour voice): Now I
believe you worked for Bowyer's Sausage Company
between . . . er . . . (*she rustles the papers and looks up
with a sweet smile*) . . . in 1973?

JIM (*uncertainly and looking at the CU member, who shrugs*):
Ye-es. That's right.

LADY (*still smiling encouragingly, as you do to a new small
child in a large school*): And is it not true that you
received free sausages from time to time?

> (*A silence. The chairman sits fingertips judiciously
> balanced against each other. He is a lawyer. The trades
> council representative is comfortably settled, eyes half-
> closed. The Claimants Union supporter is open-mouthed,
> getting the drift of the argument; Jim has cottoned on
> too.*)

CU That was three years ago. And it was part of the job. Mr
Perks was earning a poverty-line wage anyway. He needed
the meat for his children on those wages. he worked long
hours and did overtime for Bowyers.

JIM: Not half I did.

CU: Anyway, it's not relevant. This appeal is about clothing.

LADY (*smiling, still sweet*): I repeat—is it not true that you
did receive from time to time, as an *extra*, free sausages?
(*The words 'free sausages', especially emphasised, hang on
the air.*)

JIM: Er . . . yes. Yes, I did.

LADY (*spreading her hands wide, sitting back and raising her
eyes to the ceiling*): Well, Mr Perks. (*She says this in the
manner of one who thinks, 'Well, Mr Perks, why are you
here then? If you received free sausages.' She fingers her
heavy ornamental brooch and picks up her expensive
fountain pen.*)

CU: Are you suggesting that when Mr Perks and his wife go
to the Co-op or somewhere to buy shoes and raincoats,
they tip a lot of old sausages on to the counter? And do
you think anyone will accept sausages as legal tender?
(*Thinking, you've got to tackle these people on their own
terms.*)

CHAIRMAN (*his voice impersonal and formal*): The tribunal
has made a note of all these points discussed today and

will let you know its decision in writing in a day or two.

Note: The only further appeal against the decision of this tribunal is to the High Court. Who is going to take on *that* weighty procedure, or after hearing a tribunal raise these kinds of points who is going to have any confidence in the justice or simple rationality of its decision? Certainly claimants are not going to have that confidence. What we learn from the kind of experience is that we are being handled by a system developed to protect the interests of our rulers. Even well administered—and there is no doubt that this chairman *is* administering it well—it is only well administered from that point of view and militates against the interests of anyone less rich and less powerful.

It is, for example, in the interest of our rulers to mystify claimants with complex procedure. As a rationing device, this works very well. Part of the fight back for claimants must consist in overcoming this mystification and so Claimants Union members support one another at appeal tribunals and at the local offices . . .

Scene: Plymouth Social Security Office
Date: 9 May 1978

'We're here from the Claimants Union.' About fifty faces stared at us.

'We are a group of claimants who have formed an organisation to help one another with any problems; we may be able to help if you don't feel you're getting a first-class service here.' I waved a hand towards the grills behind me and noticed in turning that they'd taken down the rack which the managers had promised us last year would be filled with every conceivable leaflet: there were just three holes in the wall and three grubby notices on an otherwise empty notice-board. So this was where that little preliminary, liberal meeting with the management had led us.

'We are here today with the book of rules, if you need any information.' A pause. I grinned and did my master-of-ceremonies.

'Is everybody happy?'

'No, we're bloody not'—a voice from the back. Everybody laughed.

A young woman on the front row caught my eye. She was pregnant. She had a small child on her lap. We went over to her. John, a social work student who had joined the union, started opening his notepad, all its pages tipped out at different levels where he'd given people information about the union meeting.

'It's the rent,' she said.

'How much do you pay?'

'Twenty-four quid.'

'When's it due?' Stupid question. She wouldn't be here if it wasn't due today.

'Today. Else she'll chuck us out.'

'Did they send you a giro?'

'They got in a muddle or something and it got lost. I had some last Saturday.'

'But now you've got no money.'

'That's right. I fed the baby this morning.'

This was *last* Tuesday all over again: no money, no food, possibly no roof if the SS didn't cough up—and a 19-month-old baby going hungry because there wouldn't be any pay-out of money until after 2.30 this afternoon.

'We'll come up with you if you like. What's your number?'

Her ticket number was 97. The number on the wall changed as we watched: 80. The room was crowded. An old lady about the height of a ten-year-old heaved herself up: shapeless shoes, a worn coat, a headscarf, no teeth, a shopping bag nearly touching the ground. She sat down in the chair at the grill: one of our old-age pensioners a lot of lip service is paid to in the media because they are deemed 'deserving', but they are going through the same troubles as everyone else, anyway.

'Call us when your number comes up.'

A man, smartly dressed in a dark raincoat, white shirt, striped tie, beckoned us over. He sat in a row of empty seats. He wore brightly polished shoes, smartly creased trousers. He leaned forward turning his ticket over and over. His hair was neatly brushed and parted, his glasses wire-framed. The air outside was sweet.

'I've not had any money for a fortnight.'

'I smelt peppermint on his breath and, faintly, alcohol.

'None for a fortnight.'

'No.'

'Have you signed on?'

'I came out of prison a fortnight ago and went into a hostel.'

'Oh. Mm.'

'It's for alcoholics. And I signed on and they sent me to these people and I haven't heard anything.'

'We'll come up with you and make a new claim.'

'Yes. Thank you.' Each word carefully measured and spoken. 'I'm going to be thrown out.' Suddenly he was near to tears. 'I haven't any money for the hostel and I had a drink yesterday.'

'You mustn't drink.' I sounded like a temperance lady in 1890. But I thought, hunger's making him drink: poverty's a killer.

'It's my number now.' We all went to the grill. I bent round one side of him and John bent round the other. We couldn't move the chair. It was screwed to the floor.

'Name? Address?'

'Well, until today . . . '

'Yes? Address?'

He gave the address he'd been at. The hostel run by churchmen who had just slung him out.

'When did you last receive benefit?'

'Well, I . . . I . . . haven't received any, you see. I never heard from your office.'

He was apologetic, tentative, hesitant. I hoped that he'd somehow find somewhere else. I still remembered a group of men who'd had nowhere to live and turned up to union meetings with notes from the SS with 'NB: If you remain NFA [no fixed abode] and do not get an address we will be unable to pay you after this week.' We had only been able to secure their money after all of us had gone to the office together, and the men had been really frightened.

John leaned forward. 'We're asking for an urgent-needs payment over the counter. Otherwise this gentleman will have nowhere to stay tonight.'

The clerk, a patient young man wearing a shining wedding ring, wrote on the white form. But we couldn't read it.

'Get a giro organised. It's after 10.30.' There was a payment at 10.30 every morning—in theory.

'We can't do anything now. The supervisor's at a meeting.'

'When they get back from their junketing upstairs then they can get on with paying out giros. So put it on her desk.'

'They won't be back from lunch until after 2.'

A group of people came through the swing doors behind us. More nightmares.

'But I'll put it on her desk. You've not been paid for a fortnight, you say?' He wrote it down.

He was the most sympathetic clerk in the building. We were lucky. It made a lot of difference.

The man got up from the screwed-down chair and cleaned his glasses. I saw his fingers trembling and thought about his comfortlessness.

'See you this afternoon.' But I didn't see him again—until a few days later I saw him in the same clothes carrying the same bag disappearing amongst a crowd of shoppers in a busy street.

A girl touched me on the arm. Could we go over to her? She'd been evicted on Sunday. She showed bruises where the landlord had thrown her out. Her friend had paid him £19 on Saturday so they had no money left and no roof either. Her friend was there too. John sat and talked to them. The police were dealing with the landlord but where had she stayed last night? She'd slept rough: at the railway station and then on the floor of her friend's mother's house. She'd not eaten either.

The friend's mother turned up later in the afternoon. She was a generous woman with a lined face and a loud laugh; but she was poor too and it limited her generosity. She knew about the union and was glad to see us.

A yellow-haired woman called me over. Her husband had been sick; now he was back at work but they would have no wages for another ten days. She's hated coming but they had three children, the rent was due and she needed money. I sat with her and we worked out what she ought to get on the back of an envelope. I told her to ask for an A124 form—I explained it was the equivalent of a pay-slip. Her number was called.

At the grill the clerk wrote down her name and address and her claim for a week's money. He said he'd go and get her papers.

'What papers?'

'Your supplementary benefit papers—in your file.'

'I haven't got any.'

'No, we have them.'

'No, you haven't.'

Deadlock. I butted in.

'This lady's family's been on sickness benefit.'

'You've never been on supplementary?'

'No.'

'You'll be interviewed then.'

'When?'

'Couldn't say. Sometime. We're booked up today.'

'Look, I'm not coming back here tomorrow. I haven't enough money. I can't keep going backwards and forwards across town.'

'Perhaps sometime today, then.'

'My children need lunch at home and my daughter here's got kidney failure but I had nowhere to leave her. She's got to be at the hospital this afternoon. I can't sit here all day.'

'Put it on the form and take it to the supervisor. She must be back from her meeting by now.'

He wrote it down. We left the grill and almost at once her name was called for an interview. That was the result of the combined effect of the three of us being there and her being able to yell: perhaps the supervisor had heard her.

We went through to the interview cubicles along the side of the building. The sun shone into each suntrap; the central heating was on still and the cubicles were like a row of little ovens.

The yellow-haired woman sat in the chair and we bent ourselves round either side of it. The young woman who conducted the interview was not the supervisor after all. She was unsmiling. It took more than ten minutes to write down the full names, ages, and address of the five members of the family; and the date her husband had last received any money from his employer (he'd had £2 about a fortnight before); whether the family had any savings and how much (they had none); how much rent they paid and to whom; the amount of child benefit they received. All this was then read aloud to us before she was asked to sign the form.

It is all perfectly standard procedure and it was dealt with unbiasedly and impersonally.

'When will I get the money?' She was holding the envelope on which we'd worked out her entitlement in the waiting room.

'All this will have to be checked and the council notified so they can verify the rent. If it is all as you say it is . . . '

'Bloody cheek.'

The clerk stared out of the window.

'As I said, if it is all as you say it is, my supervisor will make the decision about your entitlement to benefit.'

'What you need,' the yellow-haired woman said loudly and deliberately, 'is a wig and a gown sitting there like a bloody judge in court.' She looked at me and winked. I grinned. The clerk didn't and stood up.

'You'll either get a giro or a letter explaining . . . '

'I'd better bloody get the money. How else am I to feed the kids? I've got bills to pay and the rent.' She still sounded strong but she was going red and her hands were agitated.

'Don't worry,' I said. 'You're entitled to the money. You've more than paid for it in your taxes already.'

'*We* decide about your entitlement,' the clerk said and the door slid across.

We all went out.

'Well, I gave her as good as I got,' the woman said. 'Treat you like muck though, don't they? See you tomorrow, I suppose. Cheerio.'

The number on the wall now was 97. Maggie, the pregnant young woman, was turning round in the chair by the grill, waving. We went over and watched while the details were written down.

'What's the problem?'

'I got some money last Saturday because your people lost my giro last Wednesday and my landlady won't allow Annie and me,' the baby was sitting up with its bottle of sugar and water to stop its hunger, 'to stay if I can't pay the rent and if my husband knew . . . 'She petered out. When you have so many troubles they all come rushing out, as though you'd taken your thumb off the tap.

'Maggie's got no money. The baby's hungry. The landlady wants, Maggie's pregnant and needs good food herself so she needs money straight away.'

I must have been talking loudly. The waiting room was still. John leant forward explaining about the lost giro of the week before.

'So it's an urgent-needs payment,' he finished.

'If I don't pay the landlady today I'll be out.'

'I'll just see what's happened to your papers.'

The clerk slid through the sliding doors. I used to laugh to myself at all this talk of 'my papers' and remembered Pinter's tramp searching round England telling himself that his papers were safe in Sidcup. But I don't laugh any more—there were nearly a dozen people in the waiting room simply waiting for their lost papers to be found. And the length of time it was taking you could imagine they might very well *be* in Sidcup.

Exactly a week later one man's papers were found almost within seconds. Supported by the local Claimants Union he was making a claim for an urgent-needs payment plus arrears of nearly £50. Suddenly a stranger turned up at the grill and announced that he was the taxi driver who'd brought the claimant to the office. The claimant and the taxi driver agreed that the claimant needed a taxi because he was agoraphobic; the taxi driver promptly made out a bill for £7. The clerk said he'd go and look for the papers and almost instantly returned with them. Nevertheless the taxi driver— a local bouncer weighing in at about 15 stone and standing 6ft 5in high—added another 50p to take the claimant back home. He leaned over the top of the grill—not just up against it like the rest of us—and the clerk signed the bill. £7.50 would be in the post in the morning straight to the taxi driver's address. If more shopkeepers, bus conductors, removal men and landlords actually turned up at their customers' interviews the money would (it appears) be paid out more quickly; certainly the taxi driver's money was promised as though a large taxi meter were suddenly ticking in the silence of the waiting room.

The clerk came back to us empty-handed. Maggie's papers were with the supervisor.

'She'll deal with you and you must come back this afternoon.'

'I've got the ante-natal clinic this afternoon. I've got to see my doctor.' Maggie said it softly. She sounded blurred and I hoped they hadn't put her on tranquillisers—at four months pregnant. But perhaps it was just weakness and lack of food.

'This lady's pregnant,' I said again. 'She needs good food, Liver, fresh meat, eggs and cheese and fresh vegetables. She hasn't eaten yet today and she hasn't any food at home.'

I thought of Andrex adverts, Lux adverts, adverts for building societies—all of them soft, misty pictures blossoming with the fullness and sweetness of motherhood; persuading women that this was what motherhood was like; not telling them that motherhood was something different again for poor women.

Nobody had told Maggie that she could get extra money each week to cover the cost of the special diet a pregnant woman needs to build a healthy baby.

'My clothes don't fit and I need some shoes,' Maggie put in. 'Write that down as well.'

Like the yellow-haired woman Maggie's voice was gaining strength from having people there supporting her.

'Tell the supervisor about the ante-natal clinic.' John said to the clerk. He was feeling both sorry for the clerk and urgent for Maggie. Having been a social worker he understood the clerk's conflict: being instructed behind those sliding doors to enforce the policies of the office management and being faced at the counter by people's actual needs.

I didn't have the disadvantage of that particular conflict. As an unemployed married woman I felt identified with the claimant. If this lad, nice though he was personally, was prepared to follow 'their' orders to do poor people down then he had to be prepared for what came his way as part of our resistance. Because so long as there is a Claimants Union around resistance is what he and all the other clerks are bound to get.

Like Maggie I'd had children, and I was inside her skin. Her baby was due before her husband came out of prison and she was living in a boarding house coping with a small hungry child. What was she asking for?

Simply, enough to keep the two of them together in that room and to keep them alive. After her rent was paid she had £6.35 a week to feed and clothe the two of them.

At the front of the Supplementary Benefits Handbook is a sentence which reads:

> The scale rates are regarded as covering all normal needs which can be foreseen, including food, fuel, and light, the normal repair and replacement of clothing, household sundries (but not major items of bedding and furnishings) and provision *for amenities such as newspapers, entertainments and TV licences* [emphasis added].

How, I ask myself, does this last point apply to Maggie, pregnant, with a toddler, living on £6.35 a week? Or to a man recently out of prison? Or to the two girls illegally evicted? Or to the many other penniless claimants I've met during the last two and half years?

And what Maggie was asking for today was nothing beyond this £6.35. She had not received even that yet and it was last week's money.

The clerk came back. Maggie would have to wait to be seen. Would she get a giro? He thought so.

John tore off another piece of paper out of his notebook with the Claimants Union meeting place on it.

The afternoon passed. The waiting room floor was covered with broken crisps where a toddler had eaten lunch. Two teenagers alternately necked and rowed in the middle of the room. An old man had been waiting for four hours for a pension book. They'd told him they'd lost it. Last year I'd seen an old man in a similar situation, owing rent, needing to buy food for himself and his invalid wife, waiting in the heat; in desperation he'd eventually collapsed on the floor crying. It cost more getting an ambulance than it would have cost giving him his book: I hoped it wasn't going to happen again. The two homeless girls periodically went to the grill asking to be interviewed. Finally one was told that she mightn't get any money at all and there mightn't be time to interview her either. She sat and wept. Maggie and the baby had disappeared.

We were waiting with Maureen. At last she was called on the tannoy. She had been waiting for five hours. The supervisor interviewed her: a brisk lady with technicolour make-up and a charming smile which didn't touch her eyes. Maureen sat in the screwed-down chair, thin-lipped; she ran her hands through her hair. She hadn't eaten all that day at least.

The problem was explained: John did a lot of the talking because Maureen by now was tired and defeated. Her patience and quietness had brought her to the edge of a waking sleep—Exactly the state where a person is most submissive and ready to accept anything.

Eventually the supervisor agreed to pay a giro of £15. This was a victory in itself because it meant that Maureen and her two children would have a roof for the night. She looked relieved: she'd spent two nights walking around and sleeping at the station already. That was illegal, the supervisor said.

Maureen and her husband had been evicted by a 'bad' landlord after her husband had been made redundant. He was sleeping on a couch at his mother's house; she and the children had been placed in bed and breakfast by a housing official; the same housing official was going to provide them with the keys to a council house. Maureen's particular nightmare, then, was limited in time to about a month, but the next fortnight was going to be difficult to survive and she was in the middle of this bad dream right now.

The question, of course, was the cost of the boarding house. While it is the housing department's responsibility to put somebody in a house, to provide a roof over their heads, it is the responsibility of social security to pay whatever the landlord is charging.

The catch is that no one has any control over what the landlord *is* charging: the social security office won't pay beyond a fixed amount that it considers 'reasonable' in the area and the consequence is that Maggie or Maureen or you or me go hungry.

We discovered all this later. At this interview, however, the supervisor was maintaining very strongly that if Maureen had been 'put' into this accommodation by the housing department then it was the housing department's job to pay the bill over and above the amount the social security considered 'reasonable'.

'You go back to Mr Block and tell him he's got to pay the extra.'

We persuaded her to phone Mr Block to speed up the whole business. Maureen had to stay at the office another hour or so to collect her giro for £15. It had taken nearly six hours to collect that money, and all of it was going to the landlord. She couldn't be in two places at once so we agreed to go and tackle Mr Block.

I was interested to meet him. He worked in what was known as the more 'liberal' wing of the housing department. We walked there in the sunshine glad beyond belief to be out of that Kafkaesque building; we had been in it for six and a half hours.

Mr Block was standing in his open, airy, carpeted office: modern lighting, a curving counter, trailing ferns and pot plants—and seated around the walls, homeless people.

We introduced ourselves as members of the Claimants Union, but he knew John as a social worker and so his treatment of John was noticeably on a man-to-man-we-professionals-together basis. His arms remained folded on his ample stomach throughout our talk; his eyes were unblinking and he stood with his legs apart. He listened to us without moving a muscle.

He began by saying that the Dyson family had simply walked out of their original home; the landlord had denied he'd evicted them. They had walked away without any fuss; he said that the man in the case was a lot easier to deal with than the woman; that she couldn't manage because she spent money on unnecessary things.

Such as?

Well, like bathing the children. We might well laugh; but it wasn't *necessary*. The environmental officer of health had said that a strip-wash—that is, a bowl of water with a flannel—once a week was quite adequate.

No, of course that wasn't how the environmental officer

of health kept himself clean. No, of course he didn't only allow his own children to keep clean like that. But for people like the Dysons, it was *good enough*. Mrs Dyson made too much fuss about bathing the children and that was that.

He wasn't trying to throw doubt on anyone's credibility and what did I mean that it was an appalling thing to do? They might *seem* very reasonable, ordinary people to us but he'd like to tell us that he for one wasn't going to let anyone have money willy-nilly just because they or their innumerable children needed it. The country couldn't afford it.

Well, all right, he shrugged, so there were plenty of Rolls Royces about and there might be Lagondas outside the Holiday Inn but the difference was obvious: those people had money and the Dyson family didn't.

What's more (gathering steam) he wasn't going to be pushed around by me or by anyone else, so there. What's more, if Mrs Dyson came into his office as a homeless person then he was afraid that the house lined up for her would no longer be available. I concluded from that that Maureen was going to be punished for not being able to meet the landlord's bills *and* keep clean *and* eat; and for having sought the support of members of the Claimants Union.

All this time John was talking himself into the ground in an effort to show the housing officer that what he and the supervisor at social security were saying was contradictory and Maureen and her family were sliding down the gap between. The supervisor was saying that the housing department had to pay the rent which was over and above the 'reasonable' figure accepted by the social security office; Mr Block was refusing to pay anything, saying the law didn't give him any financial power and we'd have to go back to the Social security supervisor. This was going to mean in the days ahead that Maureen was either going to go mad from exhaustion taking these contradictory messages backwards and forwards between the two offices or was going to lose the council house because even if she paid the bill that night with the £15 giro she wasn't going to be able to pay it the next night.

Eventually Mr Block agreed that he did understand this contradiction and its implications and if John came with

Maureen the next day they could resume the contest; but that all this was Maureen's fault because she must be 'mismanaging' (a favourite word, I have discovered, which people on middle-class incomes apply to people living at poverty-line level).

Before we left I just had time to tell him that Maureen wasn't living wantonly by bathing her children every other day, that she couldn't stop the landlord charging 20p a bath and that no one could possible complain that too much state benefit was being paid out while £300 million—some estimates put the figure at £600 million—was lying around unclaimed because people didn't know enough about their welfare rights.

Mr Block curled his lip (it is not an ungenerous description) and expressed the opinion that he didn't ever want to see either of us again.

*   *   *

One of the easiest conclusions you could draw from these examples might be that the system isn't well administered and that if it were none of these things would happen. It is true that they all contain instances of official behaviour which are counter to the policies proclaimed by the Supplementary Benefits Commission, and nearly all contain infringements of claimants' legal rights. But this view ignores the systematic ways in which the laws themselves, and the administrative rules for their implementation, control and constrain the day-to-day lives of claimants, and restrict their opportunities for achieving more than a hand-to-mouth existence.

The six-week and four-week rules are respectively devices for punishing workers suspected of leaving employment 'voluntarily' or of 'failing to avail themselves of employment opportunities'—irrespective of the pay and conditions. These are the official counterparts of the press campaigns against 'scroungers and parasites'. The fewer jobs there are available, the more the unemployed are feared and the greater the outcry against welfare beneficiaries. Rationing by delay is simply another expression of the feeling that such claimants are both undeserving and dangerous.

The cohabitation rule forces a woman claimant to become financially dependent on a man with whom she has a relationship—instructions to special investigating officers suggest (para. 2493 of the secret AX code) that three successive nights in her home are taken as *prima facie* evidence that they are 'living together as man and wife'. The purpose of the rule is said to be so that a woman claiming social security and living with a man who earns a wage should not thus obtain an advantage over her married counterpart. But it is in line with the general rule in social security that a woman and her children are treated as dependent upon a man, and that she is not entitled in her own right unless she is living alone and 'unsupported'. The rules reinforce the status of the woman as dependent, and the man as the provider and 'head of the household'.

Similarly, controls about accommodation are to be found in official SBC policy. Paragraph 59 of the Supplementary Benefits Handbook reads:

> The outgoings of both privately rented and owner-occupied housing may be regarded as unreasonably high if the claimant is occupying èxcessively large or luxurious accommodation, or if it is situated in an unduly expensive neighbourhood.

Stylistically evasive, this passage means in practice that lists of addresses unofficially circulate between claimants, often given out by social security clerks in the first place, of accommodation so cheap that it is considered reasonable. It is all a polite way of saying that ghettoes of poor families and single men and women should be allowed to grow in inner cities. These ghettoes do exist and are growing because of state policy. Meanwhile, others are going hungry; their catering allowance has to pay the 'unreasonable' rent—a charge they cannot control.

Regulations like these express the fundamental attitudes behind our system for relieving poverty—and controlling the poor. They outline an approach to poverty that has changed little over four centuries. They enforce low-wage work, family relationships based on financial obligation, and slum housing. Until we *share* wealth, work and leisure, assume that relationships are based on love and not money, and respect each other's rights to a decent environment, none of these things will change. In turn, these attitudes cannot be altered without radical changes in our social and economic system. Our present methods for regulating the poor were born at the same time as capitalist methods of production, and have evolved with them.

What has changed over the centuries is the ability of these policies to divide the working class. Until about 20 years ago, there was a considerable degree of solidarity between workers and claimants, between inhabitants of inner city ghettoes and of other working class areas. All saw that the laws for poor relief helped keep them in poverty, and all dreaded the relieving authorities. But in the 'affluent society' governments of both parties have encouraged a mythology about poverty: that our services are adequate, indeed generous, for those in real need; that only inadequates and 'problem families' have difficulties in coping; that abuse of the system by the poor is a greater evil than the way the system abuses the poor. Hostility between workers and claimants is fostered; and apparent conflict of interests is created.

Claimants are isolated not only from other groups but from each other. They are individualised by the bureaucracy, and in their frustration they resent all the other individuals whose claims delay their own. The demands of claiming fragment their lives, and cut them off from the contacts that make life meaningful. They lose their links with non-claimants, their membership of the community. They are gradually stripped of their identities other than as claimants; their relationship with society at large becomes determined by their relationship with the welfare bureaucracies.

Claimants Unions exist to do a number of different things. In terms of policy, they stand for a revolution in attitudes towards poverty. They stand for a society in which a decent and secure life for all citizens is guaranteed by the state through the provision of an adequate income. This should be more than a remote dream; at least it provides claimants with the kind of hope and purpose that is totally lacking in the policies of both major political parties, which see the poor as burdens and threats, and which can provide them neither with the work which would enable them to participate in society nor with the unstigmatised income to live at peace with themselves and their neighbours.

Meanwhile, claimants unions provide a day-to-day focus for the lives of people who have been isolated and blamed, and a chance to reassert their rights to be treated as human beings and as citizens. They provide an organisation to do battle with those who ration and regulate them, and they break down the barriers between workers and claimants created by official policy and press propaganda. Even social security staff are the victims of manufactured antagonism. They too are low paid and their departments are badly staffed.

Claimants Unions are saying clearly that for too long too many government surveys have made clever sociological definitions of poverty and poor people but have done nothing to change the causes; have done nothing, in other words, to change an economy of which poverty is an essential base.

Obviously, the next step is to make a society not based on poverty for many and profits for a few.

Towards this end Claimants Unions need to make links with organisations that represent the interests of working people; that is, groups that show themselves prepared not simply to speak but to act. Words are not enough, as we have learnt from successive governments which have kept down living standards through cuts in public expenditure, and which create unemployment to increase profitability. The words of the official trade union leadership that goes along with these policies are not enough either.

Poor people, through Claimants Unions, and working people, through rank-and-file organisations at the grass roots, must get together and organise.

9

Radical Politics and Community Action

Marjorie Mayo

For a decade now, British governments of varying political complexions have been more or less committed to community intervention programmes, from the Educational Priority Areas, the urban programme, CDP, inner area studies and CCPs to the current partnership schemes for the inner cities. Despite all the indications to the contrary, official sponsorship of citizen participation and community action has remained on the political agenda. The White Paper on the inner cities made the commitment clear: 'Involving local people is both a necessary means to the regeneration of the inner areas, and an end in its own right.'[1]

The intention of this chapter is to examine two aspects of these developments: firstly, the shifts that have taken place in radical analysis of this changing process of state involvement in community work; secondly, the way in which these theoretical developments in our understanding have contributed to a more effective community work practice. Has the development of Marxist explanations of state intervention in the community, for example, led, as some writers have argued, mainly to a 'nihilistic' approach?[2] Or has this nihilism been far less significant in the long run than the possibilities which have also been opened up? How far have we learnt over the last decade to maximise the potential inherent in what Corrigan has termed 'the possibilities of working on the contradictions'?[3]

The state and the community—some initial reactions

Initial radical professional and student reactions to government ventures into community work and citizen participation
have to be set in context. The era of the launching of CDP
and the Skeffington Report coincided, for example, with the
aftermath of the events of May 1968 in France. The era when
it was fashionable to proclaim the 'end of ideology', and for
politicians to assure the electors that they had 'never had it
so good', was followed by recurring slumps and economic
crises. This precipitated increasing state intervention in the
economy to restore industry's falling profitability.

In addition to the response of the militant working class
this situation produced reactions from the less organised
working class, the 'welfare poor'; from sections of the
expanding state bureaucracy, the 'intelligentsia'; and from
the growing student population—all crucially affected in their
different ways by the changing pressures and shifting
opportunity structures. During the Cold War these latter
groups had been particularly isolated from traditional
working-class politics and more generally from the mainstream
of Marxist theory. The explosion of 1968 and the demands
for student and citizen participation and the growth of
community action provided a heady, if lopsided, political
initiation for these strata.

Amongst the new left radical intelligentsia there was at
the time a mood of often totally unrealistic optimism about
the possibilities for radical change—it was argued, for
example, that 'red bases' could and should be established in
British universities as a prelude to wider revolutionary action.
This extraordinary radical optimism was coupled with a
pervasive scepticism, not only about the nature of the state
and officialdom, but also about traditional organisations and
political parties of the left which were considered to have
sold their radicalism for some mess of participatory gestures,
incorporating them ever more effectively in the suffocating
embraces of the state and the ruling class. One of the most
popular posters ran:

Je participe   Nous participons

Tu participes   Vous participez
Il participe   Ils profitent

From the other side of the Atlantic came complementary influences—not only from the student movement but from the welfare rights and civil rights movements and the critiques of the US poverty programme. The spontaneous movement of the angry poor was contrasted with state attempts to control and to manipulate them via welfare and citizen participation programmes. The point is not that there were no elements of reality in these critiques, or even that they had no relevance in community organising. Simply, these were initial reactions set in a specific context and mood.

Not surprisingly, however, this led to an over-concentration on the social control function of the state and on the possibilities for manipulation and incorporation inherent in any state intervention in community programmes. When CDP was first set up, for instance, there were predictions of inherent conflicts of interest, with the projects being uneasily caught between the demands of governments on the one hand and those of their citizen clientele on the other. CDP workers were, on occasion, the subject of radical attack—knowing these contradictions how could they bring themselves to take on state sponsorship in community work? CDP was characterised as the government's attempt to counteract Enoch Powell's vision of rivers of blood in our cities, and to prevent the spread of US urban riots to Britain. Emphasis on the social control aspect of government programmes continues with regard to more recent initiatives, such as the youth opportunities programme.

Simultaneously, there was a tendency to romanticise and over-idealise the 'poor' and their possibilities for radical action. This was at the expense of a tighter analysis in relating the quasi-spontaneous movements of the 'poor' to the rest of the working class and the mainstream of political and social action. This was perhaps in part due to an uncritical application of US theory to the British situation, where there were already better established possibilities for labour movement involvement in community issues.

The US literature has itself also been criticised for failing to make such an analysis in US terms—notably in Hilary Rose's invaluable critique of the National Welfare Rights Movement, 'Bread and Justice'.[4] Rose illustrates how the clout went out of the poor people's movement as they failed time after time to win significant concessions. The reality of the difficulties of maintaining organisation, let alone militancy, amongst the poor stands in marked contrast to one of the myths then current that the 'poor' were relatively immune to the blandishments of state incorporation; that having no stake in the system, they would have nothing to lose and everything to gain by radical protest.

There were, of course, critics who consistently argued that the focus upon poverty *per se* was misguided, insofar as it distracted from an analysis of the context and ultimately the cause of poverty, rooted in inequality in the class structure and conflicting class interests in society. S. M. Miller, for example, consistently maintained that 'the issue is inequality, not poverty';[5] this concentration on poverty has nevertheless remained pervasive—not surprisingly, of course, given that its manifestations, the symptoms of a class-based society, have been increasing rather than decreasing.

Focusing upon the poorest members of society—those on welfare or the dole—has tremendous emotive appeal. The whole rediscovery of poverty in the 1960s was part of the liberal, humanitarian, reform-lobby approach which saw poverty in terms of falling below a minimum subsistence level; or in terms of the highest score on a range of indicators of social deprivation, as when the CDP areas were picked. The implications of this approach were twofold. To the liberal reformer the working class as a whole was in receipt of adequate income and social services and in need of no particular further attention. The focus was upon those who, through whatever personal misfortune, had fallen through the 'safety net'. There was no fundamental social structure of inequality and exploitation. To the leftist, on the other hand, the poor were the focus, as the potential source of revived radical energy in promoting social change. There was, as Coates and Silburn have argued, widespread distrust of the traditional organisation of the working class, and a prevalent belief amongst the New Left that the Labour Party in particular, but also important sections of the working class more generally, had been incorporated and embourgeoisified:

> Among many of those people most deeply and successfully involved in community work there is a considerable and profound mistrust of other forms of association. Not only is the local council execrated but so are the radical or one-time radical political parties, the Trade Unions and other associations of a functional rather than local colour.[6]

Whatever such organisations were actually achieving or failing to achieve in the field of community action, they were not the main focus of radical professional and student attention at this stage in the development of community work.

This distrust of traditional working-class politics was, of course, amplified by the performance of the Labour government after the years in opposition in the 1950s.

Student politics and then the women's movement were seen, along with community action, as ways of reaching social groups which had not yet been disarmed and incorporated, as short cuts to creating a new radical movement whilst by-passing the struggles of the traditional parties and organisations of the working class and the labour movement. There was very little, if any, sense of history or understanding of how community action such as the rent strikes of the First World War, the National Union of Unemployed Workers in the inter-war period and the squatting movement in the post-Second World War period had been part of the broader working-class movement.

Bringing community action back, from taking a short cut which by itself could only be a dead-end, into a dialogue with the mainstream of political life has been, I shall argue, the single most significant shift in radical ideologies of community action. This has been the product, itself, both of socio-economic change and of the experience of class struggle.

Ten years on

The discussion so far has been self-critical and somewhat

negative—over-emphasising perhaps the left's paranoia, on the one hand, and its romanticism on the other. What, if any, were the positive elements in this initial radical response and how have these developed since then, in terms of both theory and practice?

Developments in understanding the nature and role of the state in capitalist society

Radical theories of the state in general and the Marxist theory of the state in particular had been seriously under-developed, as Miliband argued; the theory focused primarily on the state's overtly repressive function as the tool of the bourgeoisie, without giving adequate consideration to other equally crucial activities.[7]

Since then the vast expansion and development of the role of the state in the stage of monopoly capitalism has demanded and begun to receive fuller and more precise analysis. Without going into these recent contributions in detail, which are anyway almost over-familiar now, it is important, nevertheless, to underline several themes which have had particular relevance for community work and community action.

Firstly, the complexity and the contradictions inherent in the state have been more adequately recognised. Social control is thus a far more complex phenomenon depending not simply upon the police and the courts, or upon the conscious or even unwitting manoeuvres of the state's social and community workers.

The women's movement has been particularly important in developing our understanding of these processes—the parallel being in the ways in which girls internalise their subordinate role as future wives and mothers.[8] The women's movement has developed our understanding of the ways in which the welfare state reinforces women's role as agents of social reproduction, just as the theorists of the city have been developing a similar understanding of the impact of the welfare state upon urban working-class communities as the physical site of collective consumption and social reproduc-tion.[9] The question then becomes not how the state polices working-class communities so much as how the working-class

individuals and organisations develop any conscious ideological challenge which takes their demands beyond the most
immediate reforms. In the light of such an analysis the initial
exasperation of radical community workers with the
apparently reactionary nature of many of their client organisations' demands, and with the organs of the traditional
labour movement, can give way to a clearer understanding of
the nature of the struggle to be waged. The problem is no
longer simply seen as how to resist government and particular
government policies, but how to do so as part of a longer-
term strategy to engage in the battle of ideas which has been
historically waged within the organisations and structures of
the working class and its allies.

It is precisely because the dominated are not inevitably
politically conscious of the nature of society that there is no
need to find conspiracies for overt social control lurking
behind every shift of government policy. Neither excessive
suspicion about each aspect of state intervention nor un-
qualified optimism about the radicalism of the working
class or the poor is particularly helpful in engaging in these
battles of ideas.

The second crucial development in the Marxist theory of
the state has been the recognition of the relative autonomy
of the state and the contradictions which exist within and
between different layers of government and indeed, within
the ruling class itself. The implications are obviously of
particular relevance for community work—as Cynthia
Cockburn, for instance, has pointed out in her analysis of
community action in Lambeth.[10] Even if local government
is ultimately not above or apart from the rules of the game of
capitalist accumulation, there is a plethora of lesser contradictions which allow room for the community organiser
to maneouvre.

The problem for the community worker in practice, then,
has been to understand these opportunities and to know how
to support the community's attempts to use them creatively.
For example, the flight of manufacturing jobs from older
industrial areas has presented key problems not only to the
communities concerned but also to the relevant local
authorities, which have, apart from any other consideration,

been concerned about the loss of rates which has ensued. Whilst understanding the limitations, there has nevertheless been scope for alliances between community and trade union organisations and the local authorities. The pattern of contradictions and alliances is shifting and complex, and of course there are dangers of incorporation, of being sucked into the local or central government machine, but equally there are dangers in confrontation, if the community support for it cannot be adequately maintained.

The third strand in Marxist thinking on the state which has had particular recent relevance has been the re-emphasis upon the direct economic role of the state in facilitating and promoting capitalist accumulation. This came as an important antidote to perhaps excessive concentration upon the relative autonomy of the state and upon its ideological and welfare functions in promoting the reproduction of the existing socio-economic structure of society, crucial as these concepts have been for community work. This new emphasis is apparent in the CDP report *Gliding the Ghetto*, which analyses government intervention in poverty programmes in the context of the government's industrial strategy.[11]

In this paper the problems of the British economy in the 1960s were set not in simple contrast with the preceding 'never had it so good' decade, but in terms of longer-term problems of profitability, endemic to the processes of capitalst accumulation. What was new, then, about the 1960s was not the rediscovery of poverty and urban deprivation, which were and are recurrent characteristics of our society, but rather the nature and scale of state intervention to restore profitability, through the promotion of the rationalisation of British industry—as Harold Wilson put it, 'technical change, tempered with humanity'. CDP, then, inasfar as it could be said to fit into any conscious long-term policy at all, fits not so much into a new policy of social control as into the social policy aspects of this rationalisation process. On the one hand rationalisation was to be applied, albeit gently at first, to the public sector—the precursor to the cuts in public expenditure, this was the phase when 'better value for the same resources' was the theme—an end to the 'bottomless pit' of social welfare spending in areas with high concentrations of socially vulnerable residents.

The reorganisation of local government and the National Health Service were similarly (if erroneously as it turned out) promoted as rationalisations which would lead to greater cost-effectiveness. Community development and community care were added into the package as part of the general attempt to increase voluntary contributions in the social services. Resources would then, it was hoped, be freed for investment in the directly productive sectors of the economy.

The other aspect of this tempering of technical change with humanity was that the restructuring of British industry inevitably involved 'shaking-out' surplus labour and re-investing in new, labour-saving capital equipment. The consequences of, for example, the container revolution on Docklands were, as the Canning Town CDP has demonstrated, increased unemployment, decreased family incomes and increased social problems.[12] The continued government concern with the social consequences of its own industrial strategy is, of course, a further example of the contradictions inherent in the role of the contemporary state.

The present government cannot afford to abandon either its industrial programme or its concern with the effects upon particular localities—thus the partnership schemes for the inner cities represent these on-going conflicts. The inherent tensions between the interests of the Departments of Industry, Employment and the Environment have provided a symbolic indicator of these more fundamental issues. It is nevertheless significant that both political parties support the inner cities initiative, albeit with important differences of emphasis allowing for a greater or minimal intervention in the role of the private market as the provider of employment.

In one sense the logic of the 'free' market system requires both the destruction of jobs and their partial re-creation in areas of unemployment.

Quite apart from considerations of the need for social control in such areas, there is a widespread belief that when the upturn in the economy finally comes, the labour of some of the young unemployed will again be required. The pool of the 'reserve army' of surplus labour must be kept at least partially fit for work through programmes such as 'Youth

Opportunities'. Suggestions for how to cope with those who will clearly never work again have been more varied—from retraining and dispersal to the 'grass it over' approach to the inner city.

It has been argued, then, that some of the major recent developments in Marxist theory have been of particular relevance in understanding the possibilities as well as the contradictions and constraints inherent in government and local government community work. This is not, of course, to imply that the task has been completed, merely that some progress has been made. For example, fuller understanding of the spatial nature of inequality is urgently needed—the process of uneven capitalist development and the ways in which this affects particular areas and communities.

Radical theory and radical practices

How, if at all, have the developments that have taken place affected radical community work practice? Community work would seem to be here to stay. The pressures which first led the state to set up community work and citizen participation programmes have not disappeared, and so neither has the impetus towards community intervention programmes. This is not in any sense to minimise the difficulties experienced by particular programmes, notably the CDP, and the well publicised termination of some local community development teams. At the same time the effects of public expenditure cuts have limited the activities of some voluntary organisations in this field. Nevertheless the government has remained involved—albeit with greater circumspection—as the new partnership schemes illustrate. At a local level, in spite of the cuts, the number of community workers employed by local authorities in social service departments actually increased from 268 to 381 between 1975 and 1976 (the only years for which the DHSS has so far separated the figure for community workers—but significant here because of the cuts).

The growth of community work has been matched by a greater recognition of both its radical and its reactionary potential. There is neither the great enthusiasm for community action as a new vehicle for revolutionary change nor the shunning of professional community work as a simple agency of social control. There are examples too of decreasing suspicion amongst potential clients and a greater willingness to work with community workers, together with a clearer understanding of what kind of results can reasonably be expected. For instance the Coventry CDP argued that its original concentration upon the poorest in the community led to distance and suspicion from traditional working-class organisations in Coventry.[13] Shifts in focus by the project have been part of a process of greater mutual understanding, so that labour organisations now see the Coventry Workshop, which developed out of the CDP, as a valuable resource.

Another factor leading to the lessening of suspicion and the continued growth in community work has been an increase in the number of projects set up in response to demands from the community itself. The Joint Docklands Action Group, for example, was set up with a grant from the planning authority for Docklands, the Docklands Joint Committee, at the request of local community groups. Community representatives hire the community workers and manage the project. Obviously this does not remove all potential sources of suspicion and misunderstanding—communities are not generally homogenous anyway, so that no single committee could be both totally representative and totally agreed on policy—but it does represent a shift to a more democratic structure of control.

The whole issue of alliances with the mainstream of the labour movement represents another major shift of focus in community work. Writing in the early 1970s Coates and Silburn stressed the importance of locating community action in a context larger than the welfare system.[14] Similarly some years later O'Malley, reviewing the struggles in Notting Hill, concluded: 'all the pointers to a theory and practice of expanded working class struggle bridging community and industrial struggles are there'.[15]

It would be a mistake to see this as a completely new phenomenon. There has been a long history of community and trade union alliances—from the Glasgow rent strike to the St Pancras rent strike, for instance—and these episodes of working-class history are now receiving increasing interest. In retrospect it was the attempts to 'go it alone' in the community in the late 1960s which were atypical—returning community work to the mainstream of labour movement politics fits into a more accurate historical view of working-class politics.

In the East End of London there is a long tradition of overlap between the different spheres, dating back at least to the end of the nineteenth century and early twentieth century. The same individuals emerge as having played key roles in housing struggles, attempts to organise the unemployed, campaigns for better health facilities, campaigns against particular plans for urban renewal and campaigns against racism and fascism as well as the better known direct trade union struggles. The notion of building a united trade union and community campaign to influence current decisions about the industrial future of the area appears as normal and obvious rather than as an alien construct imposed by an outside community worker.

Clearly the influence of the past does not of itself resolve inherent tensions between the different organisations and structures. The importance of relating to wider industrial and political struggles does not in any sense imply a belittling of the importance of the community sphere. Far from hanging on to the coat-tails of other organisations and struggles, the community worker can facilitate alliances only if there is a viable community base to build on. If there is no real community involvement, there can by definition be no genuine alliance anyway.

Community groups may on occasion play an important part in industrial struggles. The Lucas Aerospace Corporate Plan necessarily implied community involvement in determining priorities for socially useful products. Similarly, public sector campaigns to resist the cuts and to oppose hospital closures would have appeared to represent no more than the vested interests of the staff without the visible backing of the client community. If the tendency to widen trade unionists' focus from wages and conditions to the broader issues relating to the social impact and value of their labour continues, then community support would logically become more significant than ever.

Thus the need for valuing alliances in no way necessitates devaluing the significance of community organisations and community work *per se*. Furthermore, these community organisations will themselves remain viable and strong only if they are able to take up and deal effectively with the range of immediate issues which affect their members as well as the broader issues affecting the residents and workforce as a whole. The improvement of a particular block of flats, planning proposals which would increase traffic on the adjoining road, the provision of more adequate premises for a mother-and-baby clinic—these types of issue are in a sense the bread and butter of community work. Without some successes on such issues, however small-scale and intermittent, it is exceedingly hard to maintain active community interest and support—and without such support, of course, there is not a sufficient base for building the broader alliances on the wider issues. The community worker has, then, to attempt a balancing act between losing the community base on the one hand and losing sight of the issues with wider political impact on the other.

In practice the radical community worker may alternate between providing discreet guidance or information and overt leadership. Radical community work theory has emphasised the particular importance of this latter function. Community workers have been characterised in terms of their potential as political educators able to raise the broader issues and to draw out the larger strategic implications of immediate struggles. Even in new community groups, formed by those with little or no previous organisational experience, this professional voice will not of course be the only, or necessarily the most significant, influence. In broader campaigns involving those with greater organisational experience, particularly those who have played leading roles in the labour movement, the community workers' leadership role may be correspondingly decreased. In such a context, in an area like Docklands, debates about whether or not the community workers should exercise a leadership or a political education function may appear somewhat academic. In well-established working-class communities, reliable and competent research, information and organisational support are typically in shorter supply and hence greater demand from the community than politically conscious leadership.

Such a role may nevertheless be of value, as the history of the consultation process for the Docklands Strategic Plan suggests. Both research and organisational support has assisted the development of an alliance of community and trade union organisations within the formal participation process and beyond it in a range of related issues.

Community and trade union alliances in the Docklands

Rationalisations and dock closures from 1968 onwards directed government attention towards alternative strategies for development in the area. In 1971 private consultants, Travers, Morgan and Partners, were commissioned by the Conservative government to draw up alternative plans for the area's future. The plan produced would have legitimised a fundamental change in the function of East London. The area would have been transformed from a working-class area based on manufacturing and transport industries to a centre for the expansion of the service and tourist sectors of the capital. This plan was opposed by the local Labour authorities and by an alliance of local community and trade union groups which formed the Joint Docklands Action Group.

The next plan was drawn up by a consortium based on the GLC and the five local authorities—the Docklands Joint Committee. In response to community pressure, and in order to pre-empt negative reaction to any new plan, consultation played a much more important role in the formation of this scheme. The design and subsequent rejection of the Travers Morgan plan had resulted in some of the potentially most profitable land lying vacant for five years. It was hoped that adequate consultation could prevent a repetition of this costly delay. Under the new scheme groups had the opportunity to comment on different aspects of the plan as they were drawn up, topic paper by topic paper, via a consultative 'forum'. This included representatives of community groups, trade unions, employers and a range of voluntary bodies. The Joint Docklands Action Group asked for, and was given, a

grant to run a resource centre with funds for three members
of staff to enable community groups to cope with the volume
of planners' papers and to respond with their own proposals
for the areas' future. The central question was whether the
plan would facilitate a major change in the area's economic
base, and hence in its social composition, or whether it would
build on the existing structure so that residents and workers
would benefit. In view of the fact that the area had lost over
100,000 manufacturing transport jobs since 1961, employment was clearly the key issue for local people.

The consultation process over the strategy plan was
concerned primarily with allocating land uses—for example,
which sections of the map should be shaded in for industry.
The community groups and trade union representatives
pressed for the maximum for manufacturing industry in
order to provide jobs for existing residents and workers.
Some additional industrial zoning did take place during the
consultation process, and there was greater recognition of the
need for flexibility, so that small firms providing local
employment for women, for example, would be allowed to
remain in predominantly non-industrial zones. These limited
victories, however, were the result of pressure not only from
community and trade unions organisations but also from the
relevant local authorities.

Ultimately, the united pressure from community and trade
union groups has been more significant in the broader
struggles over the future of the area. The plan could zone
areas for industry but *per se* this did nothing either to halt
the rate of job losses from existing manufacturing and transport industries or to bring new industrial investment. Despite
its generalised marketing of the area, the Docklands Joint
Committee's interim progress report admitted that the plan's
employment targets were not being met.

The consultation machinery has provided only one outlet
for community and trade union involvement in these issues.
Whilst the consultation process was under way the Joint
Docklands Action Group was also producing a series of
reports on the underlying jobs crisis in the area, which were
used in discussion with local community and trade union
representatives. The first of these papers was discussed at a

conference in 1975 which subsequently led to the formation of the Tower Hamlets Action Committee on Jobs. In the following summer this committee provided the focal point for organising the campaign to resist the proposed dock closures on the Isle of Dogs which threatened a further 3000 jobs.

Although this campaign was temporarily successful, there were further attempts at dock closures in 1978; again these were resisted by a broad alliance of trade union and community groups. Similarly, too, the campaign operated at several levels, pressing not only the planning authority, via the formal consultation process, but also the employers and national and local government.

Struggles against closures and redundancies had of course taken place before, as had struggles over planning and community issues. The redevelopment of Docklands brought these issues together, not simply within the formal consultation process, but beyond it, in the wider and often more directly political campaigns over the area's future. At this stage, when the longer-term issues about the future of the area were linked to more immediate struggles, a broader cross-section of the community and trade union movement was drawn in, with involvement from the rank and file as well as from the leadership of these organisations.

There would seem to be several explanations for these developments. Firstly, the underlying economic situation of East London with the decline of local manufacturing industry, itself a part of the national process of industrial rationalisation, provided the context. The problems, then, were more clearly part of the wider struggle for jobs and less obviously merely those of planning and controlling property speculation and gentrification, the demons of the late 1960s. Secondly, there was leadership available with sufficient experience of struggles around both workplace and community issues. The local implications of the process of industrial reorganisation were therefore readily grasped and formed the focal point for organising.

Finally the Joint Docklands Action Group's resource centre was available to support the community and trade union movement, to carry out organisational tasks and to reinforce the case by providing research analysis and documentation—the facts and figures for the leaflets, press statements and pamphlets. All of these tasks are on-going as both the implementation of the plan and the future of the upstream docks remain on the political agenda.

Conclusion

The underlying pressures which led to the state's involvement in community work have not disappeared. Inasfar as community work programmes have potential for reducing these tensions, then, they can be expected to continue even if in truncated form. This leaves community workers with the problem of finding the room for manoeuvre within these constraints, walking on the tight-rope between incorporation and nihilistic disengagement. The difficulties of engaging in a viable strategy for radical communtiy work are great, whilst the results cannot be expected to be more than modest. Contrary to some of the illusions current in the late 1960s, community work on its own is not and will not be the front line of radical politics, although it can and does have a real and valuable contribution to make to the wider movement.

Community issues are, in any case, significant in their own right. Policies for housing, social security, health, education and leisure affect people's lives increasingly and so, therefore, does the need to struggle to make these services more relevant and sensitive. The level and form of welfare state provision does also have crucial importance for the total 'social wage' of the working class. Furthermore, community campaigns have potential for involving those like the unemployed and women at home who might otherwise remain totally unorganised. O'Malley stressed the importance of such action in Notting Hill:

> in the absence of such community-based struggles . . . a huge section of the population would remain in a political wilderness, with no sense of what socialism could mean to them and so open to the insidious courting of the far right.[16]

With the growth of recruiting by the organisations of the far right amongst the unemployed and disillusioned, there can be no room for complacency. Community work is also necessary as a defensive strategy. In the late 1970s a radical community work practice is therefore both a viable and an essential ingredient in radical political practice.

Conclusion

Radical Reconstruction

Martin Loney

> If the first phase of the so-called [industrial] revolution
> was to force all men to work, the phase we are now
> entering may be to force many men not to work.[1]

The argument of this concluding chapter is that while the
crisis in the inner city is both real and deepening, a solution
must be sought in broader political and economic changes.
Equally, without such changes, current economic trends
suggest that what we now term a crisis may, within ten years,
be viewed as a period of relative prosperity.

The inner city is as much a social as a geographical concept
and is generally ill-defined as either. To a great extent the
term is used as a synonym for areas where there are particular
concentrations of inadequate housing, unskilled and low-paid
jobs, ethnic minorities, a dilapidated physical infrastructure
and rising unemployment. None of these problems is the
monopoly of the inner city. Townsend, in a trenchant
critique of area deprivation policies, argues: 'However economically or socially deprived areas are defined, unless nearly
half the areas in the country are included, there will be
more poor persons or poor children living outside them than
in them'.[2] All that can be said for the inner city is that it
has a disproportionate number of such problems. More
particularly, and notably in parts of London, these characteristics often go hand in hand with a close proximity to centres
of wealth and power, and a highly volatile political culture.

The concern to revitalise the inner city is prompted primarily by a concern for social order, not a commitment to social justice. The growth of National Front support amongst alienated and frequently unemployed white youth, and the rising but less organised discontent of black and, to a lesser extent, Asian youth, have had far more impact on policy-makers than the concern voiced through the traditional political channels.

How else do we make sense of the Callaghan government's inner city policies? Policies which can only be understood as rational if their primary purpose is conceived of as 'political'. The proclaimed commitment to the inner city is diversionary in that it creates the impression of improvement in the face of the reality of deterioration. Symbolic in that it offers much publicised activity which fails to compensate even for the revenue loss the inner cities have experienced through public sector cut-backs. Ridiculous in that it is offered by a government which more than doubled unemployment in its term of office, saw 4.75 million people forced to draw supplementary benefits in order to reach poverty-line incomes, and reduced the proportion of taxation paid by upper-income groups. In 1973/4 the top 1 per cent of tax-payers contributed 16 per cent of all revenue, in 1976/7 they contributed only 13 per cent.[3] Contributions since then have declined further, helped by Healey's 1978 budget in which tax cuts were worth £754 a year to those earning £25,000 but only £95 a year to the average wage-earner—a gap further increased by successful Conservative amendments.

The problem with the urban programme is that its pre-occupation with the appearance of concern and activity belies its integral vacuity. The economic forces which have generated the inner city crisis can scarcely be affected by the insignificant expenditures permitted under current programmes. More particularly, there is every reason to predict a dramatic worsening of the situation.

The underlying structure of the British economy remains weak. Public sector cut-backs did not precipitate any private sector expansion; industrial output remains stagnant; the Common Market, far from helping to inject a healthy competitive edge into British industry, has accelerated the process of factory closure and 'rationalisation' and is estimated to be costing Britain £1 billion a year.[4] It is necessary only to speculate on the chronic crisis which Britain would face without North Sea oil revenue to realise that the last ten years have seen not a resolution of the economic crisis but a series of measures designed to obscure its depth and contain its impact. In an international economy in serious recession, where new investment is declining and, more importantly from Britain's point of view, increasingly selective, Britain is well placed to bear a disproportionate cost.

The likelihood of significant new investment in Britain's inner cities, in this context, is small. Without advantages in management skills, labour productivity or modern equipment, and with a decreasingly important domestic market, the British government is reduced to paying expensive subsidies to retain industry and attract new investment—a process replicated at the local level, where borough competes with borough to attract new industry and region with region. The announcement that the NEB was to finance a highly speculative venture into the development of silicone products reflects the necessity of government intervention to bolster the weak private sector. The announcement was quickly followed by a scramble for the location of the new company, Inmos. Tyne and Wear County Council opened the bidding with the allocation of £300,000 for the establishment of a micro-economic research institute.[5] In the United States the process is further advanced as cities and states write off taxes, subsidise new building, and develop new incentives to attract scarce investment and retain older factories. When the first Volkswagen factory was located in North America in 1976, Pennsylvania won the inter-state fight by providing subsidised loans, tax holidays, and capital construction worth up to $200 million.[6] The beneficiaries of this scramble are the multinationals, who, as unemployment increases, can manipulate the consequent political pressures, on local and national government, to increase the availability of work and to secure increasing freedom of movement and higher returns. The losers will be the inner cities, which do not have the resources, the infrastructure or the social facilities to compete successfully. Weber long ago observed the power of the rich in the municipal market place:

> in a community dependent on a market economy, and particularly a labour market, the have-nots may find their economic opportunities so much reduced that they will abandon any reckless attempts of taxing the haves or will even deliberately favour them.[7]

The irony of the British venture into micro-processors, Inmos, is that whatever short-term employment benefits it brings to the winning region, it represents a technology which can only dramatically accelerate unemployment. A French report, commissioned by President Giscard d'Estaing, warned that a major employment crisis could be precipitated through developments in micro-electronics which would reduce labouring requirements in many sectors of the economy—30 per cent in banking and a significant amount in other white-collar occupations—as well as accelerating the continued automation of blue-collar employment.[8] A British expert, Professor Stonier, argues that the effect of new developments will be to make 'the quest for industrial jobs a delusion and most routine office jobs will be in jeopardy by the end of the 1980s'.[9] This view is backed by research being undertaken by ASTMS, which predicts 'five million unemployed by the mid-1990s, even with expansionary government policies. In the banking and insurance sectors alone, half a million jobs will disappear, and in motor manufacturing the researchers estimate that the workforce will fall from 770,000 to 400,000.[10]

The abolition of tedious employment would be welcome if it were not that its effect would be 'to force many men not to work'. In contemporary western society status is primarily determined by the ownership of private capital or relationship to the labour market. Workers who are not protected by strong unions, or who are in declining sectors of the labour market, face low pay and inferior working conditions. Even where strong unions protect existing members from the effects of automation it will often be at the price of selling jobs and at the expense of the next generation of workers. The 50-year-old steelworker who accepts £25,000 redundancy money may regard himself as well out of it, but to the school leaver it is one less job available.

Not only will the benefits and costs of automation be allocated to different groups but no mechanism exists to reconcile the private benefits to the potential social costs or to distribute benefits equitably.

Workers respond to automation by seeking to maximise the rewards which they can gain from the new technology. That this should be a process fraught with conflict and suspicion is inevitable, for having replaced a growing proportion of workers by machinery the power of capital inevitably increases—as may the power of those workers who continue to be essential. Those who are to be replaced can only seek to block the changes or to gain a pay-off from them. If the latter tactic is followed it is at the expense of the next generation of workers; if the former, it is at the expense of perpetuating unnecessary labour.

Automation will increase the power of corporate directors in the public and private sectors. Those who lose power will be the growing army of state dependants, unable any longer to use the threat of withdrawing their labour to secure improvements in their condition. They will rely on the benevolence of government, moderated only by their own ability to engage in disruptive protests.

The government has sought to conceal unemployment by a variety of devices, including subsidising firms to keep on workers and an elaborate array of training programmes. An evaluation of the small firm employment subsidy showed it primarily to be of benefit to employers. The aim of the scheme is to encourage the creation of new jobs by promising a £20-a-week subsidy to selected firms for a six-month period. In fact a government study found that 48 per cent of the jobs would have been created anyway and 27 per cent were merely brought forward to take advantage of the scheme. The jobs were generally low-paid and overtime was frequently cut to enable employers to take advantage of the scheme. This reduced take-home pay for existing workers. As Chris Pond commented, 'not only were those taken on under the scheme on pay so low that it must, in many cases, hardly

154   *Conclusion*

have been worthwhile for them to work. Their arrival put workmates in the same position.'[11] Undeterred, the government extended the scheme more widely in the inner city partnership areas.

Another scheme, the temporary employment subsidy, offers employers £20 a week for up to a year to retain workers who otherwise would be laid off. The economic merits of such retention are unclear. After twelve months the workers can no doubt replace the enforced indolence of the factory by attendance at a skill centre, which will serve to keep them out of the labour force and hence the unemployment statistics. Without such a plethora of government programmes the unemployment figure would have passed two million by August 1978.

The unattractiveness of government programmes lies not only in their manifest inability to find people real jobs— except at the expense of displacing other labour force participants—but also in the low level of benefits which are usually offered to participants. The programmes are primarily directed at social control; indeed, Geoffrey Holland, the head of MSC, has apparantly divined that his own interest in the area stems from the miner's strike, which, reports the *Times Higher Educational Supplement*, 'seriously made him think about the limitations on the power and room for manouvre of any government'.[12] Mr Holland states: 'my favourite approach is for a period of time in which all young people are either in education full-time or in some form of training, community work or work experience'.[13] If full-time education could be extended to 19 it would no doubt have a dramatic effect on the unemployment figures, as would the less fashionable alternative of re-introducing national service. On the other hand it is hard to see any other merit in Holland's views. Many teenagers are only too happy to leave school at 16, and previously 'work experience' was something they obtained by getting a job. There is no report of any sudden enthusiasm on the part of school-leavers for non-work kinds of 'work experience'. As for the suggestion that most school-leavers could do 'community work', it reflects no more than an abysmal ignorance of the subject matter. Schemes have included sending over-lively 16-year-old boys to help elderly women with shopping and household chores, with predictable results.

The real concern is to ensure that the discipline of the factory is replaced by some alternative structure of social control over school-leavers and simultaneously to make a 'political' response to escalating unemployment. The MSC has specifically drawn attention to the danger of 'the growing number of young people who feel discarded by "the system" '.[14]

The junior Education Minister, Gordon Oakes, articulated these social order concerns quite explicitly when he told a London conference:

> With all the training and work experience in the world, some youngsters may never find a job. That is a horrifying prospect . . . a growing number of youngsters are bound to develop the feeling that society has betrayed them. Such feelings can very easily lead to crime and, *even more sinister*, can provide a fertile ground for the breeding of various kinds of political extremism. I do not think it is exaggerating to suggest that these factors pose a threat to the fabric of society potentially as serious as that of armed conflict between nations. [Emphasis added][15]

The trade union response to growing unemployment has been generally feeble. In 1978 it galvanised around the slogan of the 35-hour week. This demand appears miraculously to offer more jobs, without reducing the living standards of existing employees. How this is to be achieved without inflation, or unheard-of changes in productivity, or cost-saving cuts in the workforce, is unclear. Indeed, increases in productivity would nullify the employment-creating aspects of the campaign. In any case, when the normal working week was widely reduced from 44 to 40 hours between 1964 and 1966, almost half the potential for new jobs was absorbed in increased overtime.[16] Suggestions that overtime be cut have not proved popular: the 1978 AEUW conference rejected a motion to press the government to limit all overtime working to five hours a week, and instead passed a vague motion for a campaign 'designed to bring about a reduction in the amount of overtime working'.[17]

The demand for a 35-hour week could be defended if it was to be financed out of redistribution from dividends and ultimately, therefore, from wealth-holders. In fact, there is no evidence that the market would operate that way. Profitable and expanding sectors would grant the demand, passing on the cost in the form of higher prices which will be borne by all—including those in weakly-organised and low-paid sectors. Automation would be accelerated, with its acceptability ensured by reductions in the working week.

One effect of rapidly increasing unemployment has been to intensify divisions within the working class between the employed and the unemployed. For an increasing number unemployment is not a temporary hazard but a long-term problem. In 1977 22 per cent of the unemployed had been out of work for more than a year.[18] Large groups are transformed from independent workers to state dependents.

They are the clients of the MSC programmes condemned to largely futile make-work schemes. Those 'enrolled' in the youth opportunities programme are not paid wages, but an 'allowance'. They are not unionised and have no influence over their daily environment. Indicative of the fundamental weakness of the unemployed, those drawing supplementary benefit because of unemployment (as distinct from disability, for example) are paid at a lower rate than other long-term claimants (for a married couple this meant £4.80 less a week in August 1978). Jordan has drawn attention to the way in which the interests and condition of the increasingly marginalised dependants differ from those of employed workers, a difference readily exacerbated by the anti-popular press.[19] The victims of contemporary economic policies are held up as a scapegoat, and the lengthening dole queues interpreted as the inexorable consequence of spreading indolence. Taxation is eroding initiative and the will to work, employed workers must receive a higher after-tax income and the economically powerless must survive as best they can. It is a scenario carried furthest in the US tax revolt, where under the altruistic leadership of property developers, the middle and upper income groups are mounting a counterattack on public spending, spurred on by soaring municipal budgets

which have benefited upper-income municipal workers as
much as anybody.

It is the poor who will be the victims of the backlash. In
New York half the Hispanics and 40 per cent of the blacks
have been fired from the city's payroll, and the number of
welfare recipients has been cut by 25 per cent. Two leading
commentators on the American War on Poverty and the
civil rights movement Frances Fox Piven and Richard
Cloward, argue that 'in the absence of massive disturbances . . .
local and national business elites will succeed—as they are
already succeeding in stripping away the gains that the
impoverished working class people of the American cities
were able to win the 1960s.'[20]

America makes clear the meaning of this variant of class
politics for the inner city. Castells sums up the process:

> the growing abandonment and physical destruction of
> huge sectors of the central cities, particularly in the
> ghettos. Baltimore's Pennsylvania Avenue, Boston's West
> Point, St Louis Pruitt and Igoe etc., are symbols of the
> potential massive destruction that could happen if the
> current pattern is not reversed.[21]

In the South Bronx district of New York, and elsewhere,
landlords have taken to burning down their property in the
hope of cutting their losses by securing some payment from
the insurance companies; in the South Bronx more than
30,000 buildings have been burned and abandoned.[22]

The British inner city can offer no parallel, but the mass
squatting of Bengali families in Brick Lane, the organisation
of self-defence groups by conservative Asian organisations
(spurred on by more militant groups), the marked absence
of impartial policing in London's East End and elsewhere,
the manifest tensions in parts of Wolverhampton, the 1975
race riots in Bradford, the spectacular growth in juvenile
crime, these and other indicators point to a rapidly changing
context in many British cities.

Most remarkable in Britain is the vacuity of mainstream
politics, where the very magnitude of existing problems is
scarcely mentioned, where stale debates about law and order

substitute for programmes of social reform and where the
Labour Party is reduced to marketing its leader, a former
bank director and gentleman farmer, as an alternative to a
political programme. Britain, a rapidly underdeveloping
economic backwater, spends an estimated £150 million on
its espionage services—somewhat more than the increased
funds promised to the inner cities and a reminder of how
much our current practices and debates are still determined
by the grandeur of earlier days.

In the face of a national downturn in the economy the
inner city experiences particular difficulties and the solutions
advocated indicate how little improvement is expected. The
essence of many proposals for inner city regeneration is that
the inner city accepts its role as an increasingly marginal
sector of the economy. The London *Evening Standard*,
always at the fore in advocating a return to the dark ages
under the banner of progress, editorialises this position:

> It is no coincidence that the most intractable pockets of
> joblessness are in areas of planning blight such as East
> London and in Labour-dominated Inner London boroughs
> where local councils have played God hardest with jobs
> and planning rules.
>
> They have tried and failed. We must move back towards
> a freer labour market. Small labour-intensive businesses,
> struggling to establish themselves, must be promised a
> safe conduct through red tape; the writ of unemployment
> protection laws must be suspended for young workers'
> own good, lest bosses be afraid to hire them; the latent
> longing of many industries to recolonise the capital must
> not be hampered by rigid zoning of land or inflexible
> definitions of how existing buildings may be used.
>
> The type of unemployment problem London faces is a
> preview of the nation's in the next few decades, as tech-
> nology makes obsolete many more kinds of work. London
> can hack a path out of this thicket which the rest of
> Britain can follow.[23]

Hard-won employment protection, planning laws which
protect residential neighbourhoods against the nuisance of

unpleasant industrial processes, safety regulations, even taxation, all must be swept aside to 'recolonise' the inner city. The choice of words is interesting, for what is to be created would indeed seem to mirror the excesses of the Industrial Revolution, when a triumphant capital rode rough shod over labour. The only difference is that this time it will be done in the name of a stagnant capital apparently unable to move forward without turning the clock back.

If this scenario fails there is always a prospect of turning London's East End into an Olympic stadium. The GLC has already commissioned a £50,000 feasibility study of this option. In the meantime, eager speculators can envisage reaping the millions of pounds gathered—frequently illicitly— by their Montreal counterparts. The megalomania of that city's leadership has burdened Montreal's taxpayers for generations, though the city's unemployment figures are higher than ever—a fact unremarked by the Olympic's London backers.

Any alternative to these kinds of proposal must be situated within the context of changes in national policies directed at the reversal of the industrial decline which has had such a marked effect on the inner city. This would require a combination of import controls on the movement of capital, much more vigorous state intervention in the economy, and large-scale support for local cooperative enterprises. All of this will be dismissed as too simplistic, as ignoring the potential repercussions from foreign competitors on the one hand and the 'crisis of confidence' which would be created amongst private investors on the other.

The broad answer to these charges is, firstly, that existing policies are failing dramatically and, secondly, that Britain need not continue to provide a giant subsidy to the EEC, maintain an army on the Rhine and provide a ready market for foreign-manufactured imports. Private investment is increasingly taking place only under conditions in which state subsidies guarantee private profits. Such subsidies, nonetheless, leave private capital free to move and 'rationalise' at will as the Chrysler case demonstrated. Indeed, as the CDPs argued, government support frequently promotes such movement and rationalisation without regard to the social

cost involved.[24] Direct state intervention provides a greater
guarantee of public accountability and a more equitable
return on public funds.

Measures must also be taken to reduce unemployment,
which even with a vigorous programme of industrial expansion would remain at an unacceptable level, but any scheme
must go hand in hand with redistributive social policies
designed to create a broad measure of equality in pay and
conditions. Such measures are in any event ethically desirable
and are increasingly a precondition for social cohesion.
Programmes which seek to reduce the labour force without
being based on principles of equity and social justice will
encounter considerable difficulties. While many wage rates
remain inadequate and the dominant value system stresses
material consumption as the single most important indicator
of success and worth, schemes for work-sharing, or reductions
in overtime, are unlikely to succeed. Unless there is a commitment to redistribution and support for alternative social
values the condition of the unemployed must remain worse
than that of the employed as a deterrent to voluntary unemployment. Existing programmes not based on redistributive
principles offer low rates as part of a broader economic
strategy which seeks to reduce public-sector spending and
counter inflation by controlling wages and maintaining a
large pool of unemployed. If the employment created by
public sector cut-backs had been absorbed through work-
creation programmes offering average wages and salaries the
cuts would have been self-defeating. However, if instead of
offering teaching graduates full-time jobs as part of a programme of reducing class sizes, they can be offered a
temporary low-paid slot in a job-creation programme the
saving to the public treasury is clear—as is the loss of any
useful social contribution.

The relationship between the miserly sums offered and
the failure of existing programmes was demonstrated in the
job release scheme ostensibly designed to meet the desirable
goal of facilitating early retirement and reducing youth
unemployment. The benefits offered to those who retired
early attracted only the lowest-paid workers, freeing in
consequence only the least desirable jobs.

The achievement of a significantly reduced working week, early retirement and periodic industrial sabbaticals is well within the country's economic potential, and the capacity of automation to render increasing numbers of jobs obsolescent. This should also enable us to move increasing resources into the labour-intensive social service sector with consequent improvements in social welfare. The success of such a programme must ultimately depend on breaking the present inextricable link between labour market status and social status. If the market remains supreme, then the benefits brought by technological change will be enjoyed primarily by the affected shareholders and secondarily by the remaining workers. Sabbaticals will only be effective if they are backed by pay approximating to normal earnings and if they are part of a broader package designed to humanise working conditions—otherwise those returning from sabbaticals will experience considerable problems in reintegration into jobs which may be both tedious and subject to autocratic control.

The concentrations of delinquency, poverty and unemployment found in the inner city reflect the continuation of profound social inequalities. Even without further economic growth, redistributive policies could eliminate much of the hardship in the inner city. Redistributive policies would also undercut the decline in social cohesion experienced in many inner city areas and combat the polarisation endemic in the existing fight—frequently drawn on racial lines—for scarce jobs and housing resources.

Halsey concluded his panoramic survey of British society in the 1978 Reith Lectures with a warning about the fragility of our existing social relationships, based as they are on diminishing consensus and continuing gross social injustices. The liberty which had characterised British society was no longer secure, since:

The historical conditions which allowed this liberty also permitted hugely divisive inequalities of class and status. They bequeathed us a stratified society held together by imperial might abroad, and deference and respect for shared religious and cultural values at home. But external empire and internal social control have been losing their power to pacify without violence, leaving market success in all its weakness to justify a still unequal society. Our society cannot stand on such shifting foundations. To strengthen them we need principles and practices of social distribution which are acknowledged to be just by the great majority . . . the paramount principle of distribution must be equality . . . we need full equality of material conditions—equality of incomes, in the broad sense—as a foundation of social life.[25]

Without such a commitment to equality market forces will continue to pauperise a growing sector of the population. They will be disproportionately concentrated in older and declining areas, characterised by poor facilities and high crime rates. They will be there because those who could exercise choice left, and those who could not were moved in. We may call this an inner city crisis, but we will not resolve it until there is a commitment to resolve the more basic contradictions which permit the continued concentration of private wealth with its inevitable consequences in the spatial segregation of rich and poor.

Notes and References

Introduction

1. R. H. Tawney, *Equality* (London: Allen and Unwin, 1964) p. 31.
2. W. H. Auden, '1st September 1939' *Collected Shorter Poems, 1930–44* (London: Faber, 1950).

Chapter 3

1. See, for example, Peter Townsend, 'Area Deprivation Policies', *New Statesman*, 6 August 1976.
2. CDP, *The Costs of Industrial Change: Industry, the State, and the Older Urban Areas* (London, 1977).
3. The term 'inner city' has now become virtually meaningless. It is applied to a whole range of urban situations—including, for instance, post-war council estates in peripheral locations, and small older free-standing towns. Its function in debate is essentially ideological and not descriptive; in many cases it is used as a pseudonym for 'working class'.
4. See M. I. A. Bulmer, 'Policy, Society and Economy in County Durham, 1918–1972', *Durham University Journal*, vol. LXV, no. 3 (June 1973).
5. CDP, *The Costs of Industrial Change*, especially p. 46; North Tyneside CDP, *Living with Industrial Change* (1978); and Benwell and North Tyneside CDPs, *Regional Capitalism: a regional solution for the North East?* (1978).
6. Tynemouth County Borough Council, *Industries and Amenities* (1939).
7. Ibid.
8. Ibid.
9. Northern Industrial Group, *Considerations affecting post war employment in the North East* (Newcastle, 1943) and *Objects,*

Organizations and Methods (Newcastle, 1946). See also North Tyneside CDP, *Living with Industrial Change*, and Benwell and North Tyneside CDPs, *Regional Capitalism*.

10. Northern Industrial Group, *Considerations affecting post war employment in the North East*.
11. CDP, *The Costs of Industrial Change*, p. 46.
12. See, for instance, Benwell and North Tyneside CDPs, *Regional Capitalism; Tyne Conference of Shop Stewards, Multinationals in Tyne and Wear* (September 1977); North Tyneside CDP, *Living with Industrial Change*; and *Trade and Industry*, 4 November 1977.
13. In North Tyneside, of which Tynemouth is now a part, about 6000 new jobs were created between 1962 and 1975; 5500 of there were for women workers. North Tyneside MBC, *Report of the Chief Planning Officer to the Development Services Committee* (28 September 1976). Also Benwell CDP, *Permanent Unemployment* (1978).
14. Short of reading Marx's *Capital*, see Maurice Dobb, *Capitalism Yesterday and Today* (London: Lawrence and Wishart, 1973), and Andrew Glyn and Bob Sutcliffe, *British Capitalism: Workers and the Profits Squeeze* (Harmondsworth: Penguin, 1972).
15. For detailed information on this see the monthly bulletins of the North East Trade Union Studies and Information Unit; and the monthly issues of *Workers Chronicle*, the paper of the Newcastle-upon-Tyne Trades Council. Companies that have closed big Tyneside plants in the last three years include Plessey, Spillers, GEC, the Burton Group, UDS, and Fairey.
16. Treasury/Department of Industry, *An Approach to Industrial Strategy*, Cmnd. 6315 (London: HMSO, 1975).
17. Ibid.
18. CDP/PEC, *Workers and the Industry Bill* (1975); Benwell CDP, *Permanent Unemployment*. See also Tom Forrester, 'How Labour's Industrial Strategy got the Chop', *New Society*, 6 July 1978.
19. Northern Region Strategy Team, *Strategic Plan for the Northern Region*, Vol. 2, *Economic Development Policies* (London: HMSO, 1977).
20. *Guardian*, 18 September 1976.
21. Peter Shore, speech to the Annual Conference of the National Housing and Town Planning Council, Brighton, 3 November 1976—DoE Press Notice no. 926.
22. Ibid.
23. Peter Shore, speech to the *Sunday Times*/Calouste Gulbenkian 'Save Our Cities' Conference, Bristol, 9 February 1977.
24. *Daily Telegraph*, 7 April 1977.
25. *Policy for the Inner Cities*, Cmnd. 6845 (London: HMSO, 1977).
26. Department of the Environment, *Local Government and the Industrial Strategy*, Circular 71/77 (1977).
27. Peter Shore at Brighton.
28. Peter Shore at Bristol.

29. 'Housing Policies and the Inner Cities', *Labour Research*, November 1977.
30. *Guardian*, 7 April 1977.
31. *Sunday Times*, 10 April 1977.
32. *Policy for the Inner Cities.*
33. 'Not Much for Inner Cities', *Financial Times*, 10 February 1977.
34. *Financial Times*, 29 March 1977.
35. Robert Waterhouse, *Guardian*, 23 June 1977.
36. Conservative Party, *Small Business: Big Future* (London, 1977): CBI, *Enterprise into the Eighties* (London, 1977).
37. Northern Region Strategy Team, *Strategic Plan for the Northern Region*, vol. 2, *Economic Development Policies.*
38. *Sunday Times*, 27 November 1977.
39. *Guardian*, 26 November 1977.
40. *Financial Times*, 29 March 1977.
41. Nigel Mobbs (Chairman, Slough Estates Group), 'How to Attract Industry to the Inner City', *Municipal Review*, May 1978.
42. Harold Lever, at the opening of a conference on 'Small Firms in Inner Cities', Birmingham, 18 January 1978—from government press notice.
43. CDP, *The Costs of Industrial Change*, especially pp. 32–7; also Benwell CDP, *Storing up Trouble* (1978); and Benwell CDP, *From Blacksmiths to White Elephants: Benwell's Changing Shops* (1978).
44. Graeme Shankland, consultant to Lambeth's Inner Area Study, quoted by Sue Challis, 'Jobs—big inner city issue', *Morning Star*, 1 June 1977.
45. Richard O'Brien, Chairman of the Manpower Services Commission, interviewed on a BBC2 television programme, used the phrase 'social and economic programme' to describe the MSC's activities; he also said that the MSC was attempting to create a 'secondary labour market' parallel to the mainstream one in order to absorb the jobless—*The Money Programme*, BBC2, 28 October 1977.
46. Huw Beynon, 'The Multinational Challenge', *Socialist Voice*, no. 10 (November 1977).
47. *Financial Times*, 29 March 1977.
48. Benwell CDP, *Women, Work and Wages: Clothing Workers in West Newcastle* (1978).
49. Tyne and Wear Chamber of Commerce, *Tyne and Wear Industrial Journal*, August 1977.
50. City of Newcastle-upon-Tyne, *Business Focus*, no. (Spring 1978).
51. Ibid.
52. *Guardian*, 31 January 1978.
53. Peter Shore at Manchester, *Guardian*, 18 September 1976.
54. Association of Metropolitan Authorities, Cities in Decline (London, December 1976).
55. *Policy for the Inner Cities.*
56. Ibid.
57. Peter Shore at Bristol.

Chapter 5

1. For a short history of the Community Development Project see David Corkey and Gary Craig, 'CDP: Community Work or Class Politics', in Paul Curno (ed.), *Political Issues and Community Work* (London: Routledge and Kegan Paul, 1978). For a fuller account see *Gilding the Ghetto* (London: CDP Information and Intelligence Unit, 1977).
2. Richard Crossman referred to one of Derek Morell's papers as 'an astonishing mix-up of sociology and mystical religion', and referred on one occasion to his making 'a curiously Buchmanite kind of religious speech'—Richard Crossman, *Diaries of a Cabinet Minister*, vol. III, *Secretary of State for Social Services* (London: Hamish Hamilton/Jonathan Cape, 1977).
3. For example, Sir Keith Joseph's speeches when Secretary of State for Social Services on the 'cycle of deprivation'.
4. A DSS Working Party on Deprivation, appointed 1978.
5. Local Government Act, 1972. The 'implementation date' was 1 April 1974.
6. National Health Service Reorganisation Act, 1972.
7. Local Authorities Social Services Act, 1970.
8. *The Marshall Inquiry on Greater London*—Report to the Greater London Council by Sir Frank Marshall (1978).
9. *Regional Authorities and Local Government Reform* (London: Labour Party, 1977).
10. *Inner Area Studies, Liverpool, Birmingham and Lambeth: Summaries of consultants' final reports* (London: HMSO, 1977).
11. *Under Fives* (London: Association of Metropolitan Authorities, 1977); *The Under Fives* (London: Trades Union Congress, 1977); Central Policy Review Staff, *Services for Young Children with Working Mothers* (London: HMSO, 1978).
12. Lambeth Inner City Partnership, *Inner City Programme 1979/82* (London, 1978); Hackney/Islington Inner City Partnership, *Inner City Programme: Social Services Strategy Proposals* (London, 1978).
13. Michael Matcham, *The Role of Voluntary Organisations in Partnership, in Priorities in the Inner City*, Report on a Consultation (Birmingham Voluntary Service Council, 1978).
14. *Report of the Committee on Local Authority and Allied Personal Social Services*, Cmnd. 3703 (London: HMSO, 1968).
15. Ibid., para 21.
16. John Benington, 'Community Development Project', *Social Work Today*, vol. 1, no. 5 (1970).
17. M. A. Cooper, *Area Team Development Plan (Normanton)* (Wakefield District Council, 1978).
18. Aryeh Leissner and Jennifer Joslin, 'Area Team Community Work: Achievement and Crisis', in David Jones and Marjorie Mayo (eds),

Community Work One (London: Routledge and Kegan Paul, 1974).
19. P. Flynn, *Using Social Area Analysis to Inform the Corporate Responsibilities of an Urban Authority: the Liverpool Experience* (Liverpool City Planning Department, 1978) para 2.
20. See John Stewart, Kenneth Spencer and Barbara Webster, *Local Government: Approaches to Urban Deprivation*, (Birmingham: Institute of Local Government Studies, 1974).
21. See Llewelyn-Davies, Weeks, Forestier-Walker and Bor, *Circumstances of Families: Inner Area Study, Birmingham* (London: Department of the Environment, 1976).
22. See Paul Mansfield and Jef Smith, 'What a Reception', *Social Work Today*, vol. 5, no. 12 (1974).
23. Mary Sugden, Director of Social Services, London Borough of Hackney, in a personal communication, 1978.

Chapter 6

1. *Inner Cities of Tomorrow*—a report by the Town and Country Planning Association (London, 1977).
2. *Policy for the Inner Cities*, Cmnd. 6845 (London: HMSO, 1977) para 24.
3. Canning Town CDP, *Canning Town's Declining Community Income* (no date).
4. 'What future for inner cities?'—one-day conference held at South Bank Polytechnic, London, 23 February 1977.
5. Tory Reform Group, *Cities in Crisis* (London, 1976) p. 1.
6. Rochdale Metropolitan District Council, *Industrial Obsolescence: the Rochdale Approach* (1977).
7. R. Minns and J. Thornley, *Local Government Economic Planning and the Provision of Risk Capital for Small Firms*, CES Policy Series, no. 6 (October 1978) p. 14. For further elaboration see R. Minns and J. Thornley, *State Shareholding: the Role of Local and Regional Authorities* (London: Macmillan, 1978).

Chapter 7

1. Brian Jeffreys, 'Fords—Inside the Plant', *Solidarity*, vol. 3, no. 10.
2. Southwark Council press statement, 24 September 1970.
3. Bob Dumbleton, *The Second Blitz—the demolition and rebuilding of town centres in Swansea* (Cardiff, no date).

Chapter 9

1. *Policy for the Inner Cities*, Cmnd. 6845 (London: HMSO, 1977).
2. See J. Smith, 'Hard Lines and Soft Options', in P. Curno (ed.),

Political Issues and Community Work (London: Routledge and Kegan Paul, 1978).

3. P. Corrigan, 'Community Work and Political Struggle: the Posibilities of Working on the Contradictions', in P. Leonard (ed.), *The Sociology of Community Action* Sociological Review Monograph (Keele University, 1975).

4. H. Rose, 'Bread and Justice: the National Welfare Rights Organisation', in Leonard (ed.), *The Sociology of Community Action*.

5. S. M. Miller, 'Poverty Research in the Seventies', *Journal of Social Issues*, vol. 2 no. 2 (Spring 1970).

6. K. Coates and R. Silburn, *Poverty, the Forgotten Englishman* (Harmondsworth: Penguin, 1970) p. 233.

7. R. Miliband, *The State in Capitalist Society* (London: Weidenfeld and Nicolson, 1969).

8. See E. Wilson, *Women in the Welfare State* (London: Tavistock, 1977).

9. See M. Castells, *The Urban Question: a Marxist Approach* (London: Edward Arnold, 1977).

10. C. Cockburn, *The Local State: Management of Cities and People* (London: Pluto Press, 1977).

11. CDP, *Gilding the Ghetto* (London, 1976).

12. Canning Town CDP, *Canning Town to North Woolwich: the Aims of Industry?* (Oxford: Social Evaluation Unit, 1977).

13. Coventry CDP, *Final Report*, vol. 1 (1976).

14. Coates and Silburn, *Poverty, the Forgotten Englishman*.

15. J. O'Malley, *The Politics of Community Action* (Nottingham: Spokesman Books, 1977) p. 180.

16. Ibid., p. 169.

Conclusion

1. R. Titmuss, 'Limits of the Welfare State', *New Left Review*, no. 27, September/October 1964.

2. P. Townsend, 'Area Deprivation Policies', *New Statesman*, August 1976.

3. 'Tax Myths', *New Society*, May 1978.

4. See *Cambridge Economic Policy Review*, March 1978.

5. *Guardian*, 3 August 1978.

6. See J. Steele, 'American Commentary', *Guardian*, 4 August 1978.

7. M. Weber, in G. Roth and C. Wittick (eds), *Economy and Society: an Outline of Interpretive Sociology*, vol. 1 (Totowa: Bedminster Press, 1968) p. 352.

8. *L'Informasition de la Société* (Paris, 1970).

9. T. Stonier, 'Oiling the Wheels of a Slick Future', *Guardian*, 3 May 1978.

10. *Guardian*, 12 May 1978.

11. *New Society*, 6 July 1978.

12. P. Santinelli, 'Fighter Against Deprivation's Effect on Democracy', *Times Higher Educational Supplement*, 12 May 1978.
13. Ibid.
14. MSC advert, *Guardian*, 6 April 1978.
15. *Yorkshire Post*, 24 February 1978.
16. 'Strong Feelings for a Weak Case', *Guardian*, 13 July 1978.
17. *Guardian*, 10 May 1978.
18. D. Palmer and D. Gleave, 'Moving to Find Work', *New Society*, 31 August 1978, p. 455.
19. B. Jordan, *Paupers, the Making of the New Claiming Class* (London: Routledge and Kegan Paul, 1973).
20. F. F. Piven and R. Cloward, 'The Urban Crisis as an Arena for Class Mobilisation', *Radical America*, January/February 1977, p. 17.
21. M. Castells, 'The Wild City', *Kapitalistate*, nos. 4–5 (Summer 1976) p. 19.
22. 'The Year of the "Torch" ', *Sunday Times*, 3 September 1978.
23. *Evening Standard*, 2 August 1978.
24. CDP, *The Costs of Industrial Change* (London, 1977).
25. A. H. Halsey, 'The Social Order', *Listener*, 16 February 1978.